For my grand-children Mia and Oscar

This book shall not, by way of trade or otherwise, be lent, resold, hired out or otherwise circulated without the publisher's prior consent in any form of binding or cover other than that in which it is published.

Copyright @ David Holden 2025

The author can be contacted at dbholden6@gmail.com

INTRODUCTION

I have decided to write this book in the second half of my ninth decade as so much has changed over my lifetime that I am concerned that our young people are unaware that the accelerating pace of life has led to a diminishing sense of community, to a diminishing connection with nature and likely to a diminishing of personal resilience.

When I was aged twelve, a great-grandmother on my father's side died. Although I remember her vividly, in the year of Mary Schmich's birth the American Civil War was raging and this land of Australia was a very raw and a very empty place. With parents often outliving one or more of their children, Mary and her rural family knew what the words 'struggle to survive' meant.

This book is structured to move the reader's mind away from 21st century crowd-think into another time and place. This I attempt to do by putting down on paper the life-lines of two insignificant 19th century women who for me have become inspirational. However, to get the limited material available to me to flow as would a novel, I have taken actual events as recorded by a Winifred Condon to be the dots and have inserted my assumptions of what was thought and said at the time to join up the dots.

In the interest of reader's reading experience, the English expression and the depth of analytical thinking at the time has been elevated to 21st century level. As an example of the literacy level back then, I have included in the afterword an exact copy of a letter written by Mary Smitch to my father.

PREAMBLE

It is November 23, 1952. The mother of my mother is in such pain that she is rocking her head on her pillow. Sometime later upon hearing my own mother cry out I peek into the room again to see her standing by the bed and fanning a face in which the mouth and eyes are open. The old lady had gone - yet not quite gone as residual oxygen was continuing to utilise glucose for energy in her brain such that many cellular networks containing her memories had yet to disintegrate. Now in 2025 I am saying to myself:

If you had placed your hand on Teresa's forehead at the time, your hand might only have been a half-inch away from the files that contained images of a landscape that had barely changed since the earliest days of European settlement, might only have been a half-inch away from the files that contained images of large towns with even their main streets turning to mud after rain, might only have been a half-inch away from the files that contained images of single-roomed schools containing children of varying ages scratching numbers and letters on slate - and might only have been a half-inch away from scores of files recording the faces and mannerisms of those who were once known by many.

Teresa has an important place in my own life-story as from 1944 to 1951 my annual school holidays were spent with her in her lonely country house. For those periods of six weeks without friends, I spend each day unoccupied. With dinner already over as the night closes in, I wash my feet in water heated by a big black kettle on a fuel stove before moving to my bed by the light of a kerosene lamp. Now as I recall this apparently bleak situation, I am asking myself:

Why are those among your warmest memories? Why do they persist after all that has happened in your life since? Was it the abnormally low level of stimulation that enabled your mind to slow down sufficiently to be acutely aware of your immediate environment and to be deeply aware of your own being?

When Teresa's heart problem appeared to be terminal, a son transported his mother to our Sydney home. The old lady had sat in buses before - never in a car. At the end of her first week here, she receives a phone call from that son. When we hold the handpiece of the phone to her ear, her reaction is as if something alive was being held against her head. Although we had shown her how to open the fridge if she needed a drink, she always waits until one of us opens it. When she sees me switch a light on for the first time, she remarks on how quickly I did this as she thought that I had to unscrew something. So, here was a woman whose life had no cold drink in it, no hot shower in it, no movie in it, no way of cooling down in a heatwave - and not since her youth when she probably attended a dance did she have any music in it. It is a way of life almost all of us assume that nobody could possibly be happy with - yet I do not believe that I was unhappy for one moment of the time I spent at Teresa's place between waking to the melody of magpies in the morning to watching the changing colours of the clouds as the sun sinks over the hills in the west. Now as I write this I am thinking:

Maybe it is preferable for the average person to not be so active in the seeking of our culture's interpretation of self-fulfilment? Maybe all that is required to be fulfilled is for one's self-awareness to be where nothing much is happening? - yet it seems that our culture methodically works against our minds being able to flow free of any outside influence. Clear evidence for this is that there is at least one television in every home, a radio in even the most basic of automobiles and one must actively seek a place to dine out that is free of background music. Then there is the ubiquitous pocket-sized device that has the potential of taking over your every idle moment. With this piece of technical wizardry, our culture's substituting distraction for the inner-self experience of our ancestors is now close to being complete.

It is April 21, 2012. Of the six gathered here in the cemetery, one is a priest aged about forty years. With his Border Collie exploring the headstones nearby, a prayer opens the service. With that done, he reads the eulogy that I have written. The ceremony is brought to its conclusion by a sprinkling of 'holy' water over the headstone - with a little more over the plot following that. The headstone is of shiny black granite and the lettering cut into that granite in freshly painted gold reads:

Bernard McCaffery

Died 25/11/1891

Aged 21 years

To explain why this ceremony is being conducted for a person who died one hundred and twenty-one years before, I need to go back to January 2012 when I am scanning old headstones. Most are broken and leaning - some even lying face-up to the sky. Then suddenly on a stone which is still upright is the barely legible name of a brother Teresa spoke of - a man she called Bernie. As I raise my eyes to see a large old tree nearby, I am wondering:

Was that living thing witness to that burial of long ago? - and as you stand here surrounded by long-forgotten graves, there is a feeling of peace within you. From whence comes this peace? It is as if there is a spiritual connecting of yourself with those now long dead and to the time that they lived.

When I look down at the grave again there is an image in my head of a father, of two brothers and of two sisters. Standing where I am standing now, they are distressed by the sight of the mother on her knees screaming and clutching at the freshly dug earth. That is as it was described to me by Teresa who, at age fifteen, was a witness to that harrowing scene. Now as I stand here, I am thinking:

The dilapidation of this site before you is saying that here lies a man whose existence was of no value - yet this person who did not live beyond a mere twenty-one years must have been of immeasurable value to his family - and that family would have been deeply affected if able to foresee the state of his headstone as it is now. You cannot leave this town before organizing a replacement.

In the group on that day in April 2012 is a cousin I had not seen since 1953. As I remember him back then, I see a stunningly handsome young face above a strapping figure. Now by Bernie's grave the eighty-one-year-old Jim Cole is standing at the lofty height of his youth with a back as straight as a plank. It is as I look upon this man, that I am wondering:

What is it about this farmer who stands tall and straight and who works the land with big hands? Is it that he is unshakably courageous? unshakably honest? - and are all farmers that way? Having never lived outside of what suburbia has to offer - you like to think so.

Not far from Bernie's new headstone is one almost as new over what was once the weed-covered resting place of Ann Cole. Before she became Jim's great-grandmother, Ann arrived here in 1857 with one hundred and fifty-one other Irish girls aboard the ADMIRAL LYONS. She was Ann Donnelly then. Against every passenger's name is a column with the heading 'Calling' - and it is as I am seeing the entry 'house servant' that I am thinking:

A strange word is this 'calling'. It is as if some humans are destined to do the work that others are exempt from by some divine decree.

While it is uncertain that there be a supernatural caller, what is certain is that it was a government which was desirous of Ann

Donnelly - and it was not to be a house servant. It was the womb of this white female that this tiny population of Europeans at the bottom of Asia needed. Such was that need that the passage required from the young woman was just £1. That was a long time ago - yet for some unknown reason it was his great-grandmother's stepping from a square-rigged ship onto a Sydney wharf that haunted the sleeping Jim Cole. On every occasion the picture begins with the wharf and finishes with bones in a collapsed coffin containing dirt six feet below weeds. In his desperation for relief, Jim turns to a minister of the Mormon Church for an interpretation of this recurrent dream. It is an interpretation the man has the self-assurance in providing.

"The dream is to remind you that between the stepping onto the wharf and the burial are many years of grinding physical work and the bearing of eight children. As one of her sons would father a son who would then father you, it could be said that she wore herself out so that there could be a Jim Cole. I suggest you restore her grave."

Although the interpretative powers of those close to God are not without limits, if his hauntings are to leave him, Jim can do no less than accept the man's advice. So, today I can say to myself:

For at least another century Bernie's name will once again be legible above his grave - and as a shiny new headstone marks the once weed-covered resting place of Ann Cole, it will be for the remainder of Jim Cole's life that Ann will no longer come to him in the night.

As there is no surviving record on the whereabouts of the remains of two compatriots of Ann who were to become my great-grandmothers, I can only look out over that same cemetery and ask:

"Where are you, Nellie? Where are you, Mary?"

THE NELLIE STORY

WINIFRED MEETS ELIZA

It is on a day early in the October of 1897 that Winifred Condon is passing a collection box with the plea: FOR THE POOR OF LONDON THIS CHRISTMAS attached. It is while reading this that she is thinking here in this tearoom on George Street in Sydney:

Afraid not. At this time of the year all your sympathy will be directed towards those freezing to death on the other side of the Irish Sea.

When she sits at a table, a woman at the next table says hello. After recognising the Irish in her voice, Winifred and she chat about the lives they have made for themselves since arrival. During the chatting, the woman Winifred now knows to be Eliza Hurley mentions that she would like to know what became of an old shipmate.

"Ellen Campion and I had a special relationship. Now known as Nellie Madden, I have heard that she is somewhere in or around the town of Orange. My gammy leg prevents me from getting around much."

On her way home, an inner-voice is whispering inside of Winifred's head:

"Your creeping inertia has got to the stage where you have lost interest in that which once enthused you - and nobody seems to have much need for an aging childless woman. At this point in time - maybe Eliza Hurley does?"

9

WINIFRED MEETS NELLIE

It is on a day in the late October of 1897 that Winifred Condon is standing in front of a gate in a fence overgrown with a hedge. As the gate has dropped down from its top hinge, some force is required to push it open to reveal a timber house with its paint peeling and its iron roof and sagging guttering rusting.

The two windows fronting the street are exactly midway between the wall's corners and an entrance which is exactly in the middle of the wall. Poor houses of this vintage - symmetric as apple crates.

She steps onto veranda boards that are warping where the nails have popped to see just one chair with its wicker beginning to unravel. She knocks on the screen door before peering through the fly-proof netting.

Dark in there. Musty smell.

Upon hearing movement, she stands back for the door to open outwards to reveal what she hopes to be the endpoint of a project which began as a chance meeting with a stranger in a tearoom.

"Winifred Condon. An Eliza Hurley asked me to track you down."

"Dear old Eliza. Still alive. How did you find me?"

"The parish priest provided the address. I have come from Sydney."

"You must come in then."

It is when seated and squarely facing each other that arthritic fingers prompt the visitor to ask of the woman's health. When she replies to the inquiry, her top denture drops noticeably.

"Not much good since my man went three years back. I wish the children would get together- put a headstone on the grave."

"Tell me about your children Nellie."

"We lost Catherine in infancy. Margaret, Mary, Ellen and Bridget are married. Johanna, Ann and David are not. Ann is a Josephite nun. I know nothing of Phillip. He could a father or he could be dead. I don't expect to ever find out."

"It is not uncommon in large families that one child fails to fit in and simply walks away. It must be both bewildering and heartbreaking for the parents. Nevertheless, you would have to be pleased and proud to have a nun as a daughter."

"More than pleased. More than proud. Through Ann I feel the smile of Jesus upon this house. Tell me about your children Winifred."

"I have none."

She is staring at you with a pitying look. Say something!

"In one way this has been good for me. I believe that marrieds have as many claustrophobic moments as singles have lonely moments."

The woman's face is saying that she is not as convinced as her guest is about that.

As Winifred is wondering what to say next, Nellie moves the conversation on to an unforgettable experience shared by every escapee of rural Ireland.

"I often wonder how we survived the passage out."

"I have also wondered about that same thing. At one time I thought that I had arrived at an answer by observing horses. These animals feel pain and fear as we do - but they lack the self-awareness to suffer as we do. If a horse feels a weight on his back he will run until what he is carrying signals to stop - or until his heart stops. He cannot feel sorry for himself as we do. He cannot hate his pain as we do. He cannot perceive a future nor perceive a past - yet a fear of a perceived future misfortune or the mourning of a loss can drive a physically comfortable human to suicide. I believe that we survived those dreadful ships because we developed the flat minds of animals."

The woman is looking at her visitor as if wondering from where in her brain all this came from. You had better change tack.

"Were you collected by a nominator at the wharf - or did you end up in the immigration depot for hire?"

"I struck it lucky at the depot. The man who chose me was a good man. The duties not demanding. It was at his place that I discovered that I easily connected with nature and with the blacks - and it was there that I met my future husband."

When Nellie moves to the kitchen, Winifred looks around the room she is in.

So empty and so basic. All houses have small photographs on the shelf above the fire-place - but photographic studios cost money. Nine children cost even more money.

As Winifred is beginning to feel a bit uncomfortable about her own wealth, Nellie arrives back from her kitchen. She has two slices of fruit cake and a pot of tea. Following some small talk on cakemaking, the conversation gets back to questions and answers.

"How do you fill in the day now that the house is empty of other people?"

"Not empty. My son David is still here. Even if he was not with me, I do not believe that I would have a problem as I have my religion which turns what could be just an existence into something more than that - and people of my age have a lot of memories."

"If you have a pen, a bottle of ink and a few sheets of paper, I could put down a sketch of those memories for Eliza."

"I would like that."

KILKENNY

One's life story begins with the first inhalation of air - yet Nellie can still experience it as the air she is now inhaling has the same smell of leather in it.

Small and bent - you have always assumed that your father would look like most cobblers. Thin and drawn - you have always assumed that your mother would look like any woman would look after losing seven of her issue of eleven before any had reached just three years of age.

Although the workshop in the front room has BOOTMAKER displayed on the window, no boots are made. They are merely repaired. Behind the workshop is where the family cooks and eats. From here a staircase takes the family to where all are to sleep. It is on most days upon returning to a home where the walls are never free of damp and the mortar is crumbling, that Nellie has the same thought:

No matter where you be in the future, the one lasting memory of this house of your childhood will be this door to this narrow street with 1743 cut into the lintel.

With her three younger brothers, Nellie helps on her father's brother's tenancy about a half-mile out of town. As her father's trade cannot fully provide for his family, potatoes to feed twelve are grown on the stony parts. Growing in the best soil are the oats which pay the rent. Her uncle Tim's acres are just two of about one thousand in the district owned by the one landlord - and it is out of that one thousand that his tenant Fergus Clooney manages about two hundred - and it is out of those two hundred acres that Clooney sublets as many portions as he can. This arrangement enables him to collect in rent from almost one hundred men like Tim an amount far more than what the legal tenancy costs him. Contributing to the rent from the oats will be the eventual sale of two pigs. Safe from thieves they are kept inside after dark where they are noisy and rapidly fill their bedding of weed with excrement. As pork will never to be tasted by a Campion, it is on more than one occasion that Nellie hears her inner-voice whisper:

"There is a desperation of men like Clooney to exploit. There is a desperation of those who must have a patch of ground to survive. Desperation and exploitation - linked as if in leg-irons."

Helping on the farm is an enjoyable pastime for the children. Nevertheless, the struggle to survive is always to be living under a grey cloud. As nowhere in rural Ireland are the minds of even children not aware of that cloud, it came to be that one such child asks her uncle a grown-up's question.

"Tim. Does a falling into arrears with the rent worry you?"

"What could cause me to fall into arrears? Here - feel that muscle."

"It is hard."

"Now feel this other muscle."

When she says that it is also hard, the man smiles and pinches her cheek.

How you love that face with a clay pipe always stuck in it - and you must pray every day for this man whose hard muscles keep at bay the feeling that there is a rat gnawing on your innards - and you must pray every day for Jenny his tiny wife who laughs with a kind of cackle - yet sings with a pure and melodious voice songs that are not of lament - nor of rebellion - but of young love. It was Jenny who said to you when about aged six that an Ellen you may be - but to her you are a Nellie. Then everybody called you Nellie -even your own mother.

While with the passing of time images of life in Kilkenny get fuzzy, memories of feelings hang on as intense as at the time of the feeling. One never to be forgotten is how she felt seeing her ever-cheerful uncle crying as he digs under the decaying stinking foliage.

"Not one tuber worth eating. What are we to do? Pray my darling child. God listens to the prayers of the innocent."

With every potato patch in the district in ruin, it is from that day that hunger becomes every tenant-at-will's constant companion - but that was not all there was of the misery. A tenant-at-will has no legal right to resist when the landlord orders the legal holder of the tenancy to run livestock on the land with hired help. As a clearance requires that the legally unprotected tenants-at-will who are evicted have no reason to remain as squatters, it is when Tim looks at the destruction of what once sheltered his family from a cold snow and an even more miserable rain, that he is thinking of the fat landowner who cruelly turned that shelter into rubble. With ruined potato fields now covering the land, it is in Nellie's attic that twelve bodies bed down. Although the evicted family of Timothy Campion will not be clinging together in an icy rain - the sorrow is great - and it is in this relentless sorrow that an inner-voice at times raises Nellie's spirits.

"Only to Satan will the black souls of absent English landlords and their Irish opportunists be of value." [see N1]

It was sometime in the winter of 1847 that Nellie wakes to see only mother at the fire. As she sits beside her, the mother's focus remains on the flames for some minutes before she breaks her silence.

"Da's gone. We have no coffin for him."

As only his matted hair is showing, Nellie lifts the covering to expose a face with no life in it - and it is while experiencing the strange sensation of live lips on a dead forehead, that she is hearing her mother's voice in the background.

"It might be too late for him to receive the last rites. His soul may have already departed his body. Nonetheless, I have sent one of the boys to notify the priest."

That evening the family and some neighbours gather around a shrouded form supported by four chairs. In the flickering light of two candles supplied by the church, Nellie stares at the shroud.

That be your soulless father in that bag.

Next morning the grass is wet from the previous night's rain. Fragments of the remains of others can still be seen in the reopened five-year-old grave. Wishing not to see her own father with a quarter-pail of lime being dropped on top of whoever is there, Nellie's eyes are closed as she stands with the family about ten feet from the muddy hole. Upon hearing the plopping sound, she looks up to the sky and speaks to it.

"What are our lives coming to when the head of the family is now in a shared grave without a coffin?"

That night few words are spoken before all drift off to their bedding. It is as the hours are slipping by that images of her father randomly pop in and out of Nellie's head. This train of thought is abruptly stopped by a tapping on the window just above her bedding at the end of the attic. She looks up to see a face which seems to be saying something. In the morning - while saying nothing - she is tormented by an inner-voice:

"Who could that woman be? What was it that she was saying?"

Not until that evening does she realise who it must be.

That is the face of St. Catherine to whom you have been praying since receiving her picture from Aunt Jenny - but what was it that she was trying to tell you? Was it that Da would soon be out of Purgatory? Was it that he is already in Heaven? [See N2]

In the two months since her father's passing, the struggle to survive seems to be drawing closer to its fatal conclusion. London has failed to send the Indian corn meal to be distributed at no cost. To the most wretched that means the workhouse. After the first sight of such an unexpectedly large building had stopped the family on the spot, five almost emaciated humans mindlessly move step-after-step towards the entrance from where they crossover into the receiving room to join about twenty-five others. As Nellie adjusts her awareness to what she sees before her, she is suddenly struck by the significance of the moment.

Behind is the life you have known it to have been. Now here in this overwhelming intimidating environment, you are likely to live out whatever remains of it.

In the female section it is adult to this side - child to that side. In the adult group it is younger women to this side - older to that side. With the suddenness of this breaking up of the family, a tightness is gripping Nellie's throat as she carries her gown into the washroom where she is roughly stripped and scrubbed by a deeply pocked-marked woman of about forty years. Now wearing the gown, she is led by a second woman of about thirty years to a bench upon which a heavy fabric is to be made into sacks for the oat harvest - and it is there that she receives a command so threatening in tone as to quicken her heart.

"You are not to move from this spot right here. Not one inch. Somebody will be arriving to instruct you."

This sadness in you is as deep as it has ever been in your life. It seems that you struggle to stay alive just for one more week to struggle to be alive for the week after that - but what is the point of that struggle? If dead you would already be in Paradise - or would you? Maybe the Lord requires this one last trail?

On this first day, Nellie in her weakened state is barely able to stand at the end of the four hours left in it before relief comes when the older and more intimidating of the two overseers orders all the new arrivals to follow her upstairs to where they are to sleep. As every bunk has been occupied by previous arrivals, there is straw on the floor provided for any additional people.

Smells as if it has come from a farm - and so small in area.

"How many will be sleeping here?"

"All five of you."

"That means there will be a space about the width of a girl's shoulders. One or more will always attempting to get more than her fair share of the straw. Like suckling pigs, the weakest will be pushed aside by the strongest."

"Do not complain. Do not ever, ever complain."

Be careful. This woman could enjoy making your life even worse than it is now.

They are then led to the mess where some type of swill is being heated in a tub.

"Ladies. What you see and smell is stirabout - and what is so grand about stirabout? - it is food in here which is not out there."

A disturbed night's sleep is brought to a sudden end by the clanging of a bell declaring the time to be six hours after midnight. A bowl of stirabout and bread begins the working day of shifting position every few minutes seeking relief for aching muscles as fingers gradually stiffen in their struggle to stitch.

The house rules are so cowering. To break one could mean nothing in the stomach for two days. Your life is that of a wild animal whose whole existence revolves around getting something into that stomach.

Such was the existence of Nellie Campion and her mother until about four months after the family's admission when another brother of Nellie's father learned of her family's plight.

His name is Anthony. It is strange that Da never mentioned the name. Maybe due to this brother becoming man of means while he became a bootmaker? The church advises those searching for lost articles to pray to St. Anthony for their recovery. As nobody could be more lost than your mother and yourself, is there a connection? Whatever, in the shop is the boot-making Tim Campion and in the space left by his deceased Jenny is your mother. Your own father's widow is now his brother's woman! Two years ago, you would not have believed it possible. Desperate relationships form quickly in desperate times.

As she was not to see her brothers again, that time when the family split-up continues to grieve Nellie.

At the time of admission spindly limbs and sunken eyes were saying that whoever has such afflictions is already beyond saving. Sad it is to be still alive with a hole already waiting to be dumped into. That may be - but your brother, your father, Aunt Jenny and her children are now together in the Kingdom of the Lord - and if not already there - then close to moving to there from Purgatory. Such were their trials in life. [see N3 and N4]

THE PASSAGE

It is out of the din coming at Nellie from every direction that her ears pick up a voice which sends a shot through her.

"The CATARQUI. Nearing Melbourne. Over four hundred lost."

On board were young women hoping and praying just like you - and what were they thinking in their last minutes of life? What would you be thinking? You would be thinking that a million miles away is the family you have left. A thousand years ago was the time you had left them. Now we in the here-and-now leaving behind lives which barely changed are being forced by circumstances to adjust to change almost by the day before it overwhelms. What is the date today? That would be a day in the November of 1852. On the other side of the world is this colony of the crown. Said by some to be a wild place. By others to be a harmonious place. Whatever the reality, that is where the BEEJAPORE and your poor self is heading.

It is while watching this activity that Nellie turns towards a voice coming from behind her left shoulder to see what is on first impression a mass of red hair.

"Eliza Hurley. Cork. Who might you be?"

"Ellen Campion. Kilkenny. Call me Nellie."

"Well Nellie my girl. I have just seen the noticeboard for the assisted immigrants. Campion and Hurley are in the same mess of eight."

It is about five hours after casting off that Eliza in defiance of orders is climbing the steps. Nellie is following, when above her head she hears a startled voice.

"The land. It's gone!"

Strange is the sensation of standing on the top deck of such a singular object below a grey sky that is endless and threatening. Surrounded by a dark sea that is also endless and threatening.

Then a sharp and loud call from the helm to clear the deck. Now all are down to where the assisted immigrants are to spend almost every hour of their coming days.

This place known as 'between-decks' is for us maybe the best place to be. For down here we can no longer see what we feel is planning to devour us. We can still feel and hear that threat up against the hull - but we cannot see it.

The first night is one of the most uneasy the immigrant will ever have. Added to everything else that was tension-generating is the pressure of the adjacent body being felt with every movement of the ship.

It is obvious that there will never be any quiet. The air itself seems to be alive with the coughing and the sobbing.

Three feet above Eliza and Nellie are two more women whose flight from Ireland has them now jammed up against each other in a situation that only a few months before they would not have imagined they would be in - and it is here in the stern where four lamps are burning that Nellie in the bunk below is having a disturbing dream.

"When feeling down Nellie you must stop to count your blessings."

"What blessings are they ma? I have no money for when I get to Sydney. May even drown before I get there."

The tension in that scene is enough to wake her. Now with only the light of the lamps having a presence, with blanket pulled up to her chin, with knees bent so that bare feet do not stick out at the end and with body moving with the ship's continual rolling and dipping - the cold is biting as she stares out into the darkness.

Those swinging lamps are all that is keeping under control an urge within you to panic.

Nellie wakes to the sound of stomach contents being ejected and to a queasy feeling in her own. This she breathes deeply and rhythmically to calm. Moments later the hatch above the stairs is being opened to their first full day at sea. As Eliza is stirring, her messmate has a question for her.

"What in your experience is the most unpleasant sensation - pain or nausea?"

"It is nausea when you have it. Pain when you have that."

That was a silly question. You must think before asking any more. There will be times of pain. There will be times of nausea - but always will be the floor's rising and falling to remind us that for twenty-four hours of every day we balance on the edge between life and death.

However, Nellie is less concerned about what might happen and more about a floor almost completely covered with vomit. This the women mop with the sea water that men from the singles deck have bucketed down before bucketing the swill back up.

With no flow-through, it is obvious that we will be breathing fetid air until we get off this thing.

It is in the afternoon of this first full day at sea that the assisted immigrants grouped into lots of fifty are permitted at half-hour intervals to be on the top deck.

What a joy! The fresh air. The strong light. The colour blue - but the foaming green sea is making you feel more sticky than usual. With no sponge bath since leaving home - and only one change of clothes in your chest in the hold, you will be stuck with a filthy body until Sydney

As Nellie is feeling her mother's rosary in her bunk that night, an inner-voice is whispering:

"These beads. Your one familiar comfort here in this alien world."

As she begins to sob, there is a hand on her shoulder. She puts her own up to touch it - and it is as she does, that she is experiencing her first surge of affection for a woman she met less than two days before.

In this dim light of oil lamps swinging in the darkness, in this air filled with the sounds of the restless, two hands are touching - bless you Eliza.

Without turning towards the woman, Nellie has a question - it is a deep one.

"What is a life without love in it?"

"It would not be much at all my friend. Many on board have their spouse with them. Some have their children with them. All we singles have is a memory of what once was and a hope that love will be found where we are going."

"I am having remorseful thoughts of a mother praying for a daughter she will never see again. It is as if the daughter was already in a grave in Kilkenny."

"I suppose that love for one's children overwhelms all personal needs. The drive for a better future overwhelms love for one's parents. That seems to be the nature of it. The decision I made to leave my family was the best I could make. One cannot choose to be wiser than what one is at the time a fateful decision is made. Feelings of guilt must not be harboured. They will not assist in your survival."

That word 'survival' will be looming large in your mind here in a container which could be driven helplessly onto rocks - even roll over in a big sea - but the crew assisted by our prayers just might be enough to keep this man-made object between ourselves and oblivion moving in the direction all want it to keep moving in.

After thirty days on this tiny island in an endless and empty sea, all clothes and bedding are damp from the degraded caulking.

Clammy skin one can adapt to as it is constant. There is no adapting to intermittent torture. They are in our bedding, they are in our clothing and they are in our hair - lice! Our tormentors must love it down here.

The assisted immigrants are eating salt pork, black bread, lentils and oatmeal. Boiling water for brewing tea and washing utensils having to be fetched from the galley. To keep the sides of the ship clean, only the use of those privies on the leeward side being permissible.

"Eliza. I am worried that there will be an epidemic of flux during rough weather. If we are not able to access the privies, the buckets will become full to the brim."

"My main worry is that the fresh water will become rank before we make any landfall. I have been informed by a salty old seafarer that a nauseating stink is nothing like the misery thirst is. Keep praying to your saint Nellie."

You are now fully aware that it will be Eliza's soothing of your fears that will get you through one day after another of being rocked and rolled about like flotsam, through one day after another of laboured breathing in the close air, through one day after another of lack of bodily movement - and through the entire voyage before it permanently reshapes your mind.

As when breezeless in the tropics that sleeping room under the stars on the top deck is only for the families, Nellie is confined with the singles to the oven below. The abnormal stillness is intensifying an unease that has been with her from the moment she stepped on board.

"Since the seas to which we are heading were described to me as being terrifying, I have been struggling to remain calm. Could they be that bad?"

"It is true my little messmate. Once past the Cape there is no large land mass to calm the wind swirling around the Antarctic. We will also be travelling far south to get the strongest of them. They will be freezing. Bad times ahead Nellie."

It had been a lucky ship weatherwise until two days out of Rio when in a rostered group on top, Nellie is more than usually disturbed by the pitching of the ship, by the sound of the sails straining against their sheets and by the creaking of the yards. Then a call to go below. Now all watch the carpenter extinguish the lamps to remove any risk of fire. It is in the sudden blackness that all below are hearing the hatch being battened down as a deep gloom descends over the nearly two hundred minds as if just the one mind. Some are huddled together around the table - others are just lying in their bunks. The ship is now moving so violently as to cause the floor to be gradually layered by the stinking spills from the buckets.

The bad times predicted by Eliza have arrived. There are always sounds within the timbers and of water against the hull. Sounds that the passengers have come to associate with getting closer to Sydney. Now the groaning timber seems to be saying that this ship has only seconds to live. You may not be able to see that raging sea - yet it is terrifying enough down here in a blackness which seems to amplify both the sound and the fear.

"Eliza. There is so much wailing by so many. The sound of it is increasing my own fear."

"It has the same effect on each of us - but the wailing would only be here on the singles' deck. Mothers on the marrieds' deck would have been quietly weeping while trying to calm their children."

All wake on the fourth day since the wildness hit to what they say is a heavy sea. Cheerful chatter is emerging along the length of the deck. By mid-afternoon the rhythmic movements through the water are back. Now the chatter sounds even joyful.

The ship seems to be sound. All have survived. The storm has completely blown itself out. Our prayers have been heard.

All occupants from between-decks are now crowded on top while gunpowder is burning below to sweeten the obnoxious odours.

There is a buzz in the air as if the storm never happened. Sucking fresh air into lungs and turning faces to the warm sun has done that - yet below waits an unwelcome task by order of the ship's surgeon. As the floors are to be scrubbed with vinegar - hands will be raw.

As the days following the storm come and go, all on board can do nothing but accept their fate confined as they are on this manmade object under an endless sky and surrounded by an endless sea as it moves towards a destination seeming to be an endless distance ahead.

"Eliza. Although human adaptation seems to be a magical thing, I still wonder why we have not lost our minds."

"You did not lose your mind because you are in the company of others who share the same misery - yet share the same belief that every ordeal has an ending. It is in this sharing that the individual draws strength. The shared experience is saving your sanity as it is surely saving mine."

Although the days drag by, there is no end of opportunities for Eliza's sanity-saving chatting - even for some theatre. One of note involved a red-headed woman of about twenty years and a more formidable-looking opponent as much as six inches taller. Upon hearing the ruckus at the far end, Nellie joins the spectators at that moment when there is a call to the one named Polly to go for the other's nose. It seems to have been the right call as the large woman pushes the smaller off to reveal a bloody and shocked-looking face. The smaller one's eyes are glaring as if anxious for more action. Eliza turns to her messmate.

"Best fight so far. So many achieve nothing. Not this one. We have a winner. When this ship gets to those wilds of Sydney we hear of, this little Polly will be able to look after herself."

By day sixty there had been only one burial at sea. Now that young adult back then is to be followed by a child.

You are saddened by any death - but you are grieved when the angelic goodness of a small child becomes cold and inanimate. No box in the ground and no stone marker above. Just a pitiful small bundle to be swallowed by a vast sea.

Two days after that first child there is another. Three more following five days after that and two more a day after that.

Seven gone in nine days! Every parent on board must be terrified. You know that we are on this earth to be tested - yet the death of the very young does not seem necessary in any testing.

Troubled by this thought, Nellie turns to her mentor.

"Have you ever wondered why God's dealing out of death is so random? Some dying aged a day. Others not departing until aged over eighty years. There seems to be no purpose to this."

"I have never wondered that at all, Nellie. I see the same randomness afflicting the plants, the insects, the fish and the birds. What living thing gets to die today seems not to be decided by any God. The day you die just happens to be your day to die."

Now Nellie is remembering that she has not observed Eliza utter a single prayer.

Is it possible that this woman you admire so much does not believe in God?

While awaiting tenders to take the assisted immigrants to the quarantine station, words cannot describe what had been so often imagined - yet in this elation there is an irritation. Although the water had become undrinkable a day before dropping anchor, raw throats have been left waiting for water to be delivered.

"Eliza. Have you heard anything of the organisational failure to get water to us?"

"The problem has nothing to do with incompetence my innocent friend. In the eyes of quality, those who take to the sea one deck above the happy home of bilge-rats are not real people." [see N5 and N6]

28

SYDNEY

In the hiring room of the Hyde Park depot those girls without nominators are sitting along the walls. Those seeking servants to hire are chatting on the floor.

"For centuries your family's and my family's blood remained in Ireland. Now here on the far side of the globe and under rag-like dresses, that same ancient blood is coursing through our veins. My friend. We live in historic times made possible by the chronometer, by more accurate maps and by more sea-worthy ships."

Nellie does not ask Eliza what a chronometer is as her attention has been captured by the man who is looking in her direction and by the man he is speaking to. She can clearly hear what that man says back to him.

"Your wife would approve. That girl is as plain as piecrust."

It is always upsetting to be reminded of a face you can do nothing with. To put rouge on your cheeks is to become an object to be laughed at - yet maybe the wife will be cautious in her approval of this servant's presence. There are men who prefer youth over appearance. As you will be about twenty years younger than the wife, your piecrust face may not be enough to protect you from some unwelcome interest.

The man extends his hand.

"Tom Peabody."

"Ellen Campion. Call me Nellie. I believe that you will find me to your satisfaction if your offer is to my satisfaction."

After the signing out, it is at the door that Nellie turns to see Eliza for what is probably the last time.

Most of the singles already had a friend or relative with them when they stepped aboard. Without Eliza appearing almost out of nowhere soon after your boarding, you would likely to have had nobody.

As the steam-assisted schooner moves towards the harbour's opening before turning to the south, Nellie is looking over at the BEEJAPORE as it gently bobs on the water.

Within that hull occurred events that are now over and done with. The difference between one's past and one's present can be a line as abruptly defined as the single step from the oak of a ship made on one side of the world onto the eucalypt of a wharf made on the opposite. Peabody is not saying anything. You should initiate something.

"Sir. I am surprised at the energy this far-flung settlement has. So many ships lying in the harbour. A line of masts along the docks. I am just as surprised that most buildings are of stone or bricks. The forests outside of Sydney Town must be vast."

"They are vast - but much of the timber is hard against which an axe edge and a saw's teeth quickly dull. Because of this problem - beginning as early as the previous century brickmaking has become a major industry. Where I am taking you has much of the colony's remaining soft cedar. It is remarkable that there are such trees still standing after years of unbridled logging."

Now through the heads and into the open sea, the rocking sensation the immigrant is well familiar with begins - but this time she and her employer are seated on the deck.

"This sun is really beating down. Although my bonnet may be stained and battered, I surely need it now."

"As I was born here forty hot summers ago, I can assure you that you need the best of bonnets to protect that pretty face. I will see what I can do about that."

Why did he have to make the 'pretty face' remark? Whatever, you are now seeing a man who moves like a man of forty would move - yet with skin that looks old for forty. Maybe due to those forty hot summers? So, your employer is aged forty - and that is what he would be. Back home few had anything but a rough idea what theirs was. At baptism the local parish priest would record a date that may be weeks after an unrecorded birth. Now here in the colony of New South Wales, at a time assumed to be twenty-two years after your birth, you are to be employed in the only available occupation for an Irish Catholic female. You are to become a servant in the house of a Protestant for the Protestant Ascendency in your subjugated country has been transported intact to this colony. Nevertheless, you are free. Not to be forgotten are those women who were transported here. Poor souls! Even after seven years of servitude are still destined by their status to be of such little substance as to be unable to rise above it.

THE ILLAWARRA

It was following an uneventful passage that master and servant arrive at one of the localities identified on a map of the Illawarra district. Here in Fairy Meadow is a scattering of buildings in the strip between escarpment and sea.

"Sir. There is almost nothing that looks like a meadow here. I am sure there are no fairies."

"I have no idea where the name came from. The district holds over four thousand people. Quite a few of that number are of your faith. The Protestant dominance is not as it was in your birthplace. Here a Catholic can own as many acres as he can manage. The common adjustment problems Catholics and Protestants share in a strange climate and landscape has diminished much of the division between us. Please call me Tom."

In a gesture which eases her tension a little, the master stands aside to allow the servant to enter the cedar-clad house which has a wide veranda on three sides with its entrance facing the sea. Now before her is a woman's face that is round and radiant.

"Elizabeth. Who might you be?"

"Ellen Campion. Call me Nellie."

The mistress touches the servant's hand.

"Well, Nellie my girl. I want you to regard this home as your home."

Upon meeting the three boys and one girl ranging from fifteen years to nine, Nellie notices that all wear crafted boots and tailored clothes.

"Elizabeth. It's a good life here for children. Year-round benign weather. Food in abundance."

"My girl. It's going to be just as good for you."

In the remaining daylight, Nellie wanders about the property.

The air has a brightness and a clarity to it that seems to enhance the sharpness of outline and the vibrancy of the colour of every object in view. You could raise a family here. There is nothing more that you want to do.

It is the next day that her duties begin at the site of a big copper tub situated about thirty feet from the house. When the water is just hot enough to not scald, the agitating with a wooden poker begins. With that done, there is the wringing of the heavy wet material by hand - and with that done, there is the rubbing with a bar of soap on a corrugated board any garment that is stained.

One thing of the many that separates the landed from the landless would be washed clothes. Seldom was a garment of any member of your family washed. The washing of clothes meant remaining in bed until they dried.

Next, she is introduced to an activity not ever seen performed. Before the garment is laid out flat on the table, the ironer is placed in the coals in the kitchen stove. Then with a thick cloth over the handle, this great lump of iron is raised to a height of about four inches to be plunged down. Then up-down, up-down, up-down, up-down - by which time the ironer may need reheating. To be pressed are the shirts the master wears when doing business, the frilly collars of the two females of the house and those tablecloths and curtains which look rumpled after washing.

You now understand why Peabody wanted younger arms than his wife has for this job. This ironer is heavy.

It is by the end of the week that Nellie is into a routine in which Elizabeth likes to do all the cooking. Taking care of the animals are Peabody, his children and a black boy. A fowl yard of two dozen birds is to be looked after by the new house servant.

The caring of the chooks has brought back to you how good it felt in the Old Country to be out of your father's shop and beside your beautiful uncle Tim working his two acres.

After the passing of a second week since arrival, Elizabeth asks the servant to assist at the next cake sale at St. Michael's. She notices the young woman's slight hesitation before agreeing.

"My girl. The churches in these settlements are the hubs of society. The places to be seen if one wants to assimilate broadly."

"I am reasonably confident that it be permissible for me to help with the sale of cakes in an Anglican churchyard. What is not permissible is for me to enter a non-Catholic place of worship."

"It is sad that you think like that. That ruling of your church does nothing to ease the tension between your religion and mine. No worries my girl. I know you to be a true Christian."

So, now you know that you are a true Christian. High praise indeed! While in the eyes of the Anglican it is not possible to be an honourable and upstanding person if not a Christian, our priests tend to favour the word 'suffering' as if the sufferer is assumed to belong to a higher order of humanity than the honourable and upstanding. What is not an assumption is the very real higher order of humanity that a happily married couple are. You have always assumed that lives are only fully shared when minds in addition to feelings are being shared. Now Tom and Elizabeth reaffirm that. You can only pray that what you are witnessing in the behaviour of this couple will largely define your own marriage. Marriage! Always it is there at the back of the mind. Very often in front.

It is on a day in mid-March 1853 that Nellie has her dress and drawers up to the knees and is wading into the sea before an oncoming wave sends her running back. Now sitting on the sand, she can see that the boy she came with is at the end of the beach.

He seems engrossed in what he has found down there.

She pulls her dress and drawers thigh-high.

They must be the whitest legs any human could have.

She lay back to feel the zephyrs moving over her skin after they have been warmed from their moving over the golden sand.

Everything about this country seems to be saying that for the young this is the very best time and place to be free.

Then she feels a nudge as she is hearing the words:

"Better go back now."

How long have you been asleep?

That evening the skin on the tops of her legs is becoming tight. She shows them to Elizabeth.

"My girl. I know what to do. All we Peabodys have been sunburned at one time or another. The trick is to keep the air away with butter."

Although uncomfortable, Elizabeth's 'trick' works well enough until the time to wash the butter off before going to bed.

You had no idea that this could happen. So red and painful to the touch.

Then three days later.

Your skin is peeling off!

"Nothing to worry about my girl. It is all natural - and there is something else. The skin under the peeling is a light brown. When I peeled there was only white underneath just waiting to be scorched red again. I will not put myself in that situation again."

Neither will you. The experience at the beach was almost spiritual. You must do this again - but this time being aware of the time that was passing.

Eight days after the first experience, the opportunity arose for the boy and Nellie to walk to the beach. Again, he goes down to the rocks which are at the north end - and again, she waits for him to get there before pulling dress and drawers up to the top of her thighs revealing their new colour.

Just loving the look of it. That large rock further along about ten feet from the water's edge. The tide is coming in. Until the boy returns, keep lifting the hat to check on the gap between rock and water. When the water reaches that rock. Cover up. In the meantime - get some sun on the back of the legs.

That night she waits for the redness - there is none.

You now know that with care you will not suffer again as this lily-white person from that land of lily-white people becomes as dusky as a South Seas maiden. For this you need much more time bathed by the sun - yet as each day passes confined to your duties you will be frustratingly aware of what is but a short walk away - something like a heavy drinker being frustratingly aware of the tavern a short walk away from the grip of the wife's company

After the passing of a further eight days, the boy wants to try fishing off the rocks at the north end.

"Elizabeth. Sam and I are off to the beach. Back in under two hours."

"Take young Earl along."

As the three walk the half-mile, Nellie is feeling to be well-prepared with a bottle of water, a wide cloth to lie on in her bag and a new broad-brimmed hat with a cord around the chin.

If young Earl goes off with his brother. Then for you this is going to be a good day.

As she watches the boys move off, she pulls dress and drawers thigh-high and lowers the neckline of her chemise.

Now the plan is to periodically lift your hat a little to check on the rising water's edge - also - whatever white skin that was not exposed last time must be covered sooner as you rotate like a pig on a spit every few minutes until the signal from the water's edge to cover up.

After dinner for three days, Nellie removes the mirror from the chest of drawers to move it around herself. By the third day she is delighted.

Your face may be far from being beautiful. Your skin is not. None of the pretty girls back home have this skin colour - but it is too light. It must be darker. What about Peabody's skin? His skin took forty years to get the way it is. You do not care what your skin looks like in forty years. You just like what the sun is doing now.

From then on Nellie manages to get away alone every fourth day for what are delightful April days of lying on the warm and golden sand, of splashing in the warm and sparkling water - and it is with each day in the warmth of this embrace that the extent of her nakedness increases - and it is on each day that an inner-voice whispers:

"This feeling you are having. You are being seduced by the sun."

It is by mid-May that the sun can no longer darken skin - yet the air is still warm.

The boys seem to have lost interest in accompanying you. Now nobody but you and the sea. You and the sand. You and the seduction.

It is about a half-hour after arrival on the last day in May that she is lying face down stark naked. The broad hat over the back of a head has been empty of all thought until the emptiness has two words inserted into it.

"You're rude."

The startled woman looks up to see a boy's face looking down on her. The smirking face of an older boy a few feet away. Later that night an inner-voice closes this chapter in her life.

"Brown skin that nobody sees but you. There is no point to it"

As the weeks pass since the loss of interest in the beach, Nellie is feeling the wildness of the Illawarra region seeping into her.

You would love to explore - but Peabody is claiming that as your employer you are under his protection, that it was on this understanding that London enabled you to emigrate and that it was on this understanding that the colony accepted you as an immigrant.

Then out of nowhere comes an invitation to accompany her employer to a blacks' camp.

"It is south on the shores of the big lake - between two and three hours walk each way. I want to trade one medium sized cooking pot for one, or as many as I can bargain for, decorated throwing sticks to send to England. My uncle sells such objects in his curio shop. As it seems that the head man has developed a liking for chewing tobacco, I could trade tobacco grown on the north coast for more native curios for my uncle. If so, I will be in front of where I was when it cost me a cooking pot made in Birmingham."

These people need iron utensils more than they need to spit baccy juice on the ground. Peabody seems to be just another white man passing judgement on the relative worth of a black life. It is by the white perception of what is honourable and upstanding that these first peoples are being judged, as the Indians have been judged, as the Chinese have been judged and as the Africans have been judged. Nevertheless, you will not be rejecting an invitation to discover what has been outside your boundaries.

While the master and his servant are on the south road, the servant has been too absorbed in her surroundings to think about the objective of this outing. The smell of smoke suddenly makes her aware of that objective.

You are approaching a community of people who have not emerged out of the Stone Age to even become pagan. When Peabody does his business - be careful not to stare at anybody.

Although she has made several observations, it is on the returning walk that Nellie informs her employer of the one that impressed the most.

"The blacks sit around as if there is no work to do."

"With no animals to care for, no fields to plough, plant and harvest, no houses to build, repair and clean and no clothes to wash. There is not. We whites have created a way of living which requires constant work to maintain. What do you think of the blacks generally?"

"If the behaviour of black adults is childlike, we tend to assume that they have children's minds - but we are underestimating the role a carefree culture plays in shaping the carefree mind."

"That is perceptive of you. What is not childlike is their capacity to survive without needing to degrade the ground and its water which our culture requires to define itself. I know that I am as guilty as most - but what else can I do? What else can you do?"

The man asks what else can you do. What you could be doing is whatever it takes to get to know these people better.

That opportunity came in the late March of 1854 when master and servant are near a creek entrance to the lake where Peabody and the head man are to trade. Nellie ambles over to some children where smiles exposing pure white teeth greet her. While an adult female nearby is repairing a basket, others further down are doing something around a fire. There is no man in the camp other than the head man. She leaves the children to return to her position from where she observes business being conducted by moving hands. When the negotiation ends with the shaking of those hands, in anticipation of what is about to happen her heart is pounding.

"Time to go Nellie."

"I am staying another day or so. I need a break from a life of one day just following the next - and this is my first real chance to see what I have never seen before. When I get back I will make-up the lost time."

After Peabody stares at his servant as if in a stupor for a few seconds, he is back with the head man and pointing Nellie's way while tilting his cheek onto his hand to signify sleep. Already biting into his plug of baccy, the headman seems to be nodding agreement. Now back from the 'conversation' she is feeling her master's glare digging into her.

"When away from my property I am not responsible for you."

With that parting shot, Peabody begins to walk north up the track. Nellie watches him for a few seconds before turning around to see that no one is smiling at the white woman who has been left behind by the white man.

You gave no thought to the consequences of this impulsive change in plan - yet they might simply ignore you. You have heard that which is not of their usual experience they deny exists - but do you want them to ignore you? You will need to eat something.

By the time the lengthening shadows are accompanied by an unseasonable nip in the air, nobody has come near the stranger. The headman who approved of her staying now seems to have forgotten she exists. It is as the sun had almost reached the horizon that the men appear with two wallabies, one wombat and four goannas. As each is noticing the white woman sitting over to the side, Nellie is reading disbelief on his face. When one is pointing at her, she is thinking:

What a damn fool you have been.

With the increasing darkness, the three fires with about ten sitting around each are getting brighter. When a woman comes over with a piece of hot wallaby, Nellie accepts it with her biggest smile and eyes that are asking the woman to linger - but the woman turns her back to return to the fire. Now all she can do is smile when one occasionally looks her way. It is when Nellie almost feels like crying that the woman beckons. She tentatively approaches as a space is made for her - and it is as she takes a seat that an inner-voice is whispering:

"What if a black sat down in a group of whites and just smiled, would the reaction be as welcoming?"

The chatting around the fires carries on after the meal until one by one, or in couples, the blacks wander off. The friendly woman beckons Nellie to follow her to a rock overhang beneath which is a sandy floor. Her new-found friend scrapes out a flat area to put down a mat of leaves before she does the same for herself about four feet away. Within minutes of her laying down, the woman is breathing heavily. It is while Nellie is laying on her mat that an intrusive inner-voice whispers:

"Elizabeth may not be so friendly now that she knows that you had placed her husband into a position within which he had to do what he did not want to do."

When she wakes the woman is not there.

From the position of the sun, it appears to be about one hour after sunrise. You must have been near exhaustion from emotional tension to sleep this late - and so stiff - even after a night on the ship - even after a night on the floor of the workhouse - not even then did you feel as stiff. Your back must have changed to fit six inches of feather.

After watching the men leave in the direction of the sea with only baskets, she turns her head towards the lake. When one of the three girls frolicking in the water sees her looking their way, she beckons. It is when Nellie is at the edge, that again the girl beckons. After removing her dress, the girls are giggling as they watch this person step into the water wearing as much clothing as she took off. When she squats down to shoulder level, one of the girls takes her hand and moves slowly into deeper water to where there is no sand under her feet. As she grabs the girl's neck with both hands, the girl immediately loosens those hands and places each on each of her glistening black shoulders. As Nellie gradually relaxes, she begins to float.

This is heavenly.

It seems only to have been a few minutes before the girls decide that they have had enough. Once out, they turn east in the direction of the narrow opening of the lake to the sea. Now feeling abandoned, it is as she sits in the sun to dry that Nellie reflects on those few minutes with such carefree fellow humans.

When you were alone on the beach under the sun you felt pleasure rather than joy. From this experience you have learned that it is the sharing of a pleasure that generates joy.

As she lies back for the mind to linger on an image of the experience of a short time ago, that image is abruptly replaced by an angry face which just as abruptly vanishes when an inner-voice comes to the rescue:

"Tom Peabody is not here. It is just you and a blissful silence."

Nellie wakes to see that the sun has already passed its zenith and that all the females seem to be back in camp. When she goes over to them, room is made for her in a circle in the centre of which are the plants that have been gathered. As she picks up a green berry-like object, somebody says a word. This she repeats. It is just before sunset when the fires are reduced to glowing embers that the contents of the baskets of mussels the men had gathered that day are tipped in. When cooked, Nellie's black friend flicks four out for her. It is after a dinner of yesterday's wombat that there begins a wailing and a stamping of feet - and that is when an inner-voice warns:

"*Europeans have orchestras and waltzes. The sticks and wooden tubes of these people can only make one distinct sound. What is a dance are feet which simply come down heavily on the ground. Be careful not to undervalue the white way of life.*" [see N7]

Nellie wakes feeling much better than when she woke on the previous day. The men have not left the camp - but are just sitting around talking, laughing and making faces as white children do when playing. It is on this day that she joins a gathering party of women and girls.

Learning what plants to pick and what to leave has become your most happy experience since arriving in the colony. There is only a rudimentary communication between yourself and the native - yet what there is seems to be enough to get by on.

Later when soaking her feet in the creek and beginning to hum, she notices that three men close-by have stoped their chatting.

They seem to be listening. You can sing the songs of Ireland to them. No! You will not! Different cultures create different minds. The song as you feel it would not be the song as they feel it. They may think that your rendition of The Minstrel Boy was you suffering gripe - also - you now appreciate that these people have a different sense of time. Without a calendar they cannot precisely separate one year from another. Without a clock they cannot section a day into equal parts. That these measurements to not be part of their understanding should tell your fellow whites that they simply have no need for them. To the black mind the steady movement of the sun from horizon to horizon is all that is needed to organise a working day when the one goal is to bring back something to eat before dark. [see N8]

On this her last day at a time she estimates to be two hours after sunrise, Nellie waves a farewell to black faces and broad white smiles. As she heads up the track, her mind is still mostly back where it had been for the most interesting hours of her life.

You have stepped into a culture that must have been here for millennia before whites arrived - and where you have been has generated an awakening within you - but of what good could that awakening be when escaping Ireland still did not release you from the trap you are in? As a single white woman, you exchange your labour for just enough money to survive - or you marry a man who exchanges his labour for just enough money for his family to survive. In black communities the men come together to do the one job that benefits all. The women come together to do the one job that benefits all. Nobody works for anybody or for any payment - and they spend a lot of time enjoying themselves.

It is as she moves further along the track that a feeling of concern is growing within her.

With European culture now extending beyond Europe, a community which is minimally organised is a vulnerable community. All over the globe there are simple people who are unaware of a force which can obliterate them. Driven by greed for wealth-generating land is this force. It is unstoppable because that greed is insatiable. [see N9 and N10]

The screech of yellow-crested cockatoo suddenly replaces the contemplation with a sharper awareness of where she is. Now in her head, Nellie is hearing Eliza Hurley's voice.

"The meditation of Eastern mystics is a state of not thinking. It is a state in which there is no past and no future. It is the state the minds of animals permanently occupy. It is one which is totally in the present. To enter this state in nature when walking one focuses on the physical presence that one is immersed in. Within seconds the chatter in the head would be gone. The mind is now

open to the sounds, open to the scents, open to the textures, open to the shapes and open to the colours."

It is by listening to her footsteps that she attempts to move away from her thoughts and into a sharper awareness of her surroundings.

Eliza's advice seems to be working. The air seems still - yet you feel it against your skin. There seems to be more bird calls - or were there always this many? There is a pleasant aroma in the air. Was that there yesterday - or is your nose becoming native?

As she is alone, Nellie is also aware that she is enjoying the return journey far more than the getting there. It is when slipping back into the contemplative state, that another of Eliza's wisdoms comes back to her.

"Each of us is born with a mind that is like an empty book. The range of concepts that can be written in the book has no limits. Then as we move to adulthood other paths of thinking are closed off to us by the society we live in. With experiences channelled by external forces, the once receptive mind now moves along just one road."

The former messmate's voice is now replaced with the reality of the Peabody house coming into view. Upon arrival she apologises and asks how angry was Tom.

"Not to worry my girl. Did you enjoy yourself?"

"I feel that God has smiled upon me with an experience I believe will make me a better person."

As she is saying this, that Peabody walks in. He smiles as if glad to see his employee safe.

"How did it go for you?"

If you say to him that the experience has made you a better person, he could hardly be angry.

So, that is what she said. As he is making no comment, an inner-voice is asking:

"Could you have gotten off that lightly?"

That night at dinner the master puts a challenging question to the servant who may be getting a bit too uppity for a servant.

"You now have some experience with the black way of life. Have those you saw in that encampment any chance of getting to Heaven?"

Well - do they? You have to say something.

"My position is that from the moment of my baptism I was subject to a set of rules that will get me into Heaven. Until the blacks know about Jesus, they are not subject to the rules that I am. In the meanwhile, I must assume that a black who strictly follows the rules of the tribe will also get to Heaven."

You really do not feel as if you believe in what was just said. What matters is what you did say will put an end to this probing into your beliefs.

It does not.

"According to the pope, only the soul of a person who is baptised in the so-called true church can get to Heaven. Now you are saying that the souls of the blacks could - yet if I strictly follow the rules of the Anglican Church - and I assume you agree with the pope - I cannot go where an illiterate and naked black man can go. I do not think that you know what you are talking about."

This probing must stop. Switch the focus.

"When the English oppressors took the power of the rural Irish away, we became people without purpose. Now the oppressors condemn us for being what they had made of us. If the natives are oppressed, they will become people without a purpose. Then we will condemn them for being what we had made them."

Her tactic worked.

"Please do not assume that I have not been thinking along those lines. Here we sit on land which is legally mine and mine alone - yet it was community land before I came along. Now members of that black community would be driven off by all the force I could summon from my white neighbours. That done, the whites would return to their own grants or purchases where I cannot go unless invited. If one was to seek to identify the core difference between them and us, it is that there are no fences and doors in their culture to degrade the spirit of community. The more we strive to create a society of individuals, the more the loss of community. Here are two examples of that loss. As it is the community which ensures that a black child gets the guidance he requires, there is not the negligent parent problem we whites have - and a black woman is not trapped in a house where she can be abused by the unhappy head of that household. In our white world neighbours knowing of an abuse ignore it. It is as if the space in every man's house is sacred into which there must be no intrusion. Every culture has its strengths and its weaknesses. We must be careful not to see only our strengths and their weaknesses - but I have no need to remind you of that as you have already reminded me of the demeaning behaviour of the English overlords towards the rural Irish."

Your employer is wise man. [see N11]

Nellie is not the only employee of this wise man. There is the black boy Jimmy who maintains Peabody's cows for a few pence a week and whose mother has been working as a cow-maid on several properties in the district for much of her son's life. As he has been in contact with white children from an early age, his English is good enough for Nellie and he to talk about relative beliefs. It is during one talk that she is invited on a pilgrimage.

Now you know that the feeling that he was becoming more trusting of you was correct.

It is only after a half-hour that keeping up with her pathfinder is becoming a struggle. Finally, the boy stops and points upwards at a rock face.

"Behind is a narrow gully. The home of the sacred tree."

As the climb becomes steeper, her breathing becomes heavier. It is when wondering how long she can keep going, that suddenly before Nellie is a plant with branches as thick as the trunks of some of the surrounding trees. As she gazes in wonder at this gigantic creation of nature, a black hand places a white hand on the trunk.

"Can you feel the spirit in it?"

Cannot feel anything - but there may be something there that the European cannot detect.

That night Nellie tells Peabody about the giant tree.

"I know of one greater, Nellie. Depicted in a painting of around 1827 and called The Hollow Tree of the Illawarra. It was claimed that two men and their horses could camp inside for the night."

That must be a tall tale. [see N12]

The more Nellie associates with Jimmy - the more she becomes aware of how fearful his people are of what the intruding European is doing to the land.

"This is not what God intended Jimmy. It must be the evil influence of a fallen angel my church calls Satan. Mankind must defy Satan and be kind to all creatures - even to the earth itself."

Now the boy is looking squarely at her.

"When I get a woman, I will be kind to her. You need a man miss - a kind one."

It is almost two weeks after her first contact with the tree that Jimmy and Nellie are placing their hands on that tree.

There is an energy flowing through you. Not a strong feeling - but definitely there.

As Jimmy suddenly looks south - so does Nellie - and it is as she does that, she hears the distant cracking of axes. That night as she muses on echoing axe blows invading the peace, she writes the following in her notebook:

In the still air - an echo.
They who listen with the ear hear only the blow.
They who listen with the heart hear also the cry.
But there is another sound.
Sinister and silent like an enveloping fog.
Silent to the white ear.
Loudly heard by the black heart.
It is the sound of European man on the march.
To be consumed is whatever can be consumed.
To be eliminated is whatever gets in the way.
When all has been consumed.
When all has been eliminated.
Will the march have destroyed the marcher?

Over the following weeks Jimmy and Nellie make further pilgrimages to the tree - and it is on each occasion that she feels its growing presence.

You ask as a Christian if you should be feeling such a primitive emotion - and if the logging in the area continues, should you pray for a tree? Maybe the tree is safe? To cut down our sacred tree when there were smaller trees of the same species nearby could only be because the axmen saw the job as a challenge to their destructive powers. Not because the timber was needed.

That July of 1854 ended for Nellie on a tragic note when a tearful Jimmy informs her that the sacred tree had been cut down.

This feeling you are having is so foreign. Many people that you knew have died - people with emotions. Why do you mourn the passing of a plant?

It is in her anguish that she feels an urge to put pen to paper. What she composes surprises her.

Each time I saw you I had the same wondering.
How old were you?

Before St. Patrick came to Ireland.
Maybe you were here then.
Before the first iron axe was forged.
Maybe you were here then.
But this linking of your history to human history.
That I now know to be wrong.
For all lives are but an accumulation of days.
For you - tens of thousands of them.
Just coming and going.
Yet many things made each day entirely different.
The flickering sunlight in your moving leaves.
Breezes balmy and gentle moving those leaves.
Winds cold and angry tearing at them.
Then when wet, that great trunk glistened in the sun.
This relationship with sun, wind and rain.
That was the history of your noble existence.
I will never forget that time I last visited you.
It was when I looked back as I was leaving.
And it was in a shaft of sunlight that I saw it.
Detached as they were by a light gust of wind.
A shower of dead leaves fluttering to the ground.
Now I know what I saw.
It was you waving a farewell.
So, you have gone my beautiful friend.
Gone from where you lived in peace.
Gone to where you can be at peace again.
It is in Our Lord's Eden that your pure soul resides.
The soul that I felt through my hand.

After Nellie had been practicing with Elizabeth a few basic dance steps, she is now walking towards a wooden hall with the eldest Peabody boy. At first, they see only lamps hanging from the eaves signalling that a social event is in progress. Then upon getting closer, female voices sounding shrill and male voices sounding raucous emerge through the open windows and the front door. As they step inside, a dozen or so sets of eyes point their way. When they instantly return to what they were looking at, Nellie's already high level of tension jumps to another level. Seconds later, it jumps to another level again.

Now where did he get to? There he is over there chatting with two other youths. It is obvious that you were his means to get into the place - but what are you here for? You have no confidence that your future husband will be found here when you are wearing a dress that feels to be a rag and a face that you know to be as interesting as a pudding. There are two alternatives. Step outside to wait out there in a state of dejection. Stay inside and wait in here like a lone crow on a fence.

While sitting as would a crow, agonising minutes drag by with two empty chairs to her right and one to her left. Then a smiling young woman comes over.

"You're new. My name's Judith."

Nellie's name had not left her lips before most of the woman's back has already turned away as she is excusing herself to move to a friend who has caught her attention. As deflation replaces the momentary elation, a voice calls out from the stage.

"Gentlemen. Take your partners."

Not all the escorts are on the dance floor as a few are mucking around outside - Nellie's is amongst them. Nobody asks her to dance.

Dreadful is the experience of enjoying nothing while watching others enjoy themselves. It is as if you are of no value in a gathering of fellow humans. Dances are disasters lying in waiting for the unattractive.

It is when back home that from out of her despair arises the memory of a conversation between herself and Eliza.

"Being hopeful for a man I can understand Nellie. Being desperate I cannot. Consider the single life. It is not without compensation. I have seen them. You have seen them. Married females degenerating into exhausted wrecks. So many of them."

"It is easy for you to say that, Eliza. With the thought of 'old maid' bouncing between my ears, desperate is all I can be. In the exhausted state there is some sense of fulfilment. There can never be any in being discarded. It is an existence to be dreaded."

Later when she had time to reflect with a little less emotion, she recalls something else that Eliza had to say.

"If you believe in God, then let him decide the place and time where a future husband will be found. He may not even want you to have one."

Nellie's dreaded future begins to appear to be a little less dreadful when her path crosses that of a Paddy Madden.

You had heard about men who clear virgin land and who then stay on as tenants until the owner decides to utilise the land or sell it - but the selling of the land as soon as it had been cleared does happen. It is a practice which drives the man into living in yet another temporary hut on another clearance job. Paddy has been lucky. What he cleared over a year past has not been put up for sale.

The first of him that she notices is the ruddy complexion. The second is that he dresses as if he is a still a peat-digger back in Limerick. Floppy hat with holes in it, rope holding up heavily patched trousers and boots with no socks in them.

He says that he was born in 1816. That makes him thirty-eight to your twenty-three. Age gaps of this size are common in Ireland between a young woman and an older man of some means - never between a young woman and an older man with nothing. At this moment in time, the man as a prospective partner has only one thing going for him - he is not of your gender.

As each month passes, Nellie becomes increasingly aware that the relentless passage of time was pushing her ever further into a corner - and it is on every day in September that she has the same thought.

If you are to be an accepted member of the community, if you are to avoid children pointing at you and laughing and if you are to have children of your own - it must be any port in a storm.

With a tense September behind her, the beginning of an actual friendship dates from October 1854 when the picture had become crystal-clear.

The inescapable truth is that Paddy is to be the one you will have to settle on in the brief period available to an unattractive woman of your age. Romance will have to be what others enjoy.

It takes only six more weeks of seeing the man in an increasingly better light to arrive at the day for the inevitable nervous whisper to emerge from this single woman's lips.

"Do you think we should tie the knot?"

Tears well up in his eyes. As he moves to kiss her on the mouth, she turns her head so that mouth meets only cheek.

That must have hurt him. This is a joyless courtship. Your adolescent brain had spent too much time in a fantasy world of handsome and dashing men.

The knot-tying was performed on April 26, 1855 by a Fr. Joseph Charles Sumner in the church of St. Francis Xavier in Wollongong where before him are an excited man and a woman who can only feel relieved. In the pews are three of Paddy's scruffy-looking mates and all the Peabodys. Outside, Jimmy is moaning over smoking leaves. Following the ceremony, Peabody's eldest son drives the newly-weds to Paddy's hut. Although the cart has no step, both drop to the ground without injury. As the bride is brushing off fragments of lucerne, she is looking at the marital home.

The sheets of bark on the roof are without nails to secure them. A lattice of thin saplings tied together by wire seems to have that function. As the logs in the walls have gaps between them, the inhabitants of this hut will be sharing its interior space with a whistling wind. From where you are standing there is a single glassless window with a shutter hanging off hinges made from pieces of a leather belt. Would that be the only window? It is appropriate that a fireplace of battered and rusted corrugated iron completes the picture. This structure just manages to resemble a white man's habitat.

The groom attempts to carry his bride across the threshold. When he stumbles and loses his grip, the bride manages to land on her feet. As she chuckles to relieve his embarrassment, she is noticing the floor to be compacted dirt.

From a nice room at the Peabodys' you go to this - and how out of place is the bed of ornamental iron with pink roses and green leaves on white enamelled knobs topping the posts. Paddy must be feeling proud to have a bed he assumes will impress any bride. Thankfully, the bedding looks new.

Mr. Madden is sitting on a chair as if wondering what to do next. Mrs. Madden is sitting on the bed as if wondering what to do next. Then she breaks the silence.

"I am very tied. Just want to sleep."

With cheeks feeling flush and eyes watering, the bride stretches out on the bed facing away from the groom.

You imagined better from the time you were aged about twelve. Now to be an expectation to remain forever unfulfilled. The vow to each other and to God has been made. The government paper signed. Does any unhappiness not have its genesis in unfulfilled expectations? If none do, then it follows that to be happy is not to expect much. The difference between your feelings and that of your husband on this day is living proof of that.

When Nellie wakes the next morning to see her husband slumped in the chair, she remembers her disappointment before falling off to sleep. Upon shaking him by the shoulder, the man opens his eyes to see a woman's face smiling at him. He lifts his head, straightens his shoulders and smiles back. The newly-arrived woman of the house opens what passes for a door on this first day of married life. It is a day which is beginning with an exceptionally beautiful morning.

For the first time in the history of this humblest of huts there is to be a breakfast prepared by a woman. That is going to make this man feel so good. [see N13]

Now coupled with one of the opposite gender, Nellie can fulfill what she had prayed for was to be her destiny. On December 20, 1855 twin girls arrive. Five days later is her first Christmas with a family of her own. At mass is the odd Englishman and German - the rest are Irish. The priest offers to write letters for those who cannot write. Then he speaks of his home in Cork.

You have no doubt that every mind before him is neither with him nor with God. Every mind here is with parents and siblings to be never seen again.

With the service over, the Maddens are given a lift to within a quarter-mile of their hut. The night air is balmy. The tiny babes are asleep in the slings Paddy made for them. With the wife's arm through that of her husband, she will forever remember her exact words and forever be glad they were said on a Christmas Day.

"Paddy. I have never loved you as I should. Tonight, I feel that I do."

It is early in September 1856 that Nellie suspects another pregnancy.

There will be more until such time as you are too tired of being pregnant for months - or too tired of the sex act - and what a chore that has been right from the time of the first uncomfortable experience that led to an immediate pregnancy. However, there is a memory to escape to after each ordeal. In it you are alone on warm golden sand making love with the sun. It is in his embrace that you drift into sleep.

In the months that follow, after rent and basics are met from selling timber splits there is no money left over.

Not as bad as in the Old Country. There to be penniless is to search for a dry ditch to sleep in - yet in this country this is as bad as it gets.

It is when the police are on a recruiting drive that the little family steps into a new reality. That is the joyful day that Paddy proudly puts on the uniform of a foot-constable attached to District H West. That day was March 3, 1857.

Seeing him in the uniform is generating a flashback of something said to you soon after landing on these shores. It was that the police are worse than those they arrest. Now what was said you know that you must dismiss. What matters is that your man is finally becoming someone of value. How he must be wishing that the people of Pallasgreen could see him now - yet you know almost nothing of his family - except that his father's name was Phillip and that his mother Margaret Ryan died before he knew her. Now that it is to be District H West and the town of Molong, an arduous road journey awaits the Maddens. To be of concern? Up to a point. The overriding feeling must be one of satisfaction. Life now has a firm direction and we will be living in a real house. [see N14]

THE CROSSING

The Maddens bypass the expense of the punt and ford the Nepean River to begin the climb in a dray pulled by a pair. Besides their luggage there are bails of fodder to be dropped off at two of the inns. As the fare is only £1 against the mail coach's £9, before this family are several days of exposure to the elements. Nellie with Margaret are on one side of the driver - Paddy with Mary are on the other side of him. The unrelenting discomfort is eased every hour when all can walk around a little. At one stop Paddy finds a rusted iron pick which he throws into the back. As they move on the man is silent for some thirty minutes. Then he lets forth.

"Those men of the iron gangs worked under conditions seemingly designed as much to break a man as to build a road. Ginger complexions burned to destruction. Racking muscle spasms from lifting rocks and logs. Fingers damaged from inevitable accidents. No ailment excuses a man from heavy work. He is in for a flogging if he resists. A few yards into the bush besides the road would be the graves. Buried for months while a mother is still praying for her son's survival. Thousands of miles between she on her knees and he in the ground. This road that we are on is a torturous road. Of that we now know. Built by tortured men. That is what we should also know."

"We are all anti-English Paddy. But you seem to hate them."

"My father described to me an event following the failed rebellion of '98. That be the year when the army of occupation went mad. He is aged about fourteen years at the time as he stands beside his own father. They are in a sombre group of about thirty witnessing a young man being flogged. All in the group knew him to be a man who keeps out of trouble. The story circulating within the group is that an English officer manhandled the young man's mother. As she knew that her tormenter was attempting to provoke the son, she begged him not to move. The officer kept roughly shaking her. Pulling her hair. Demanding information he knows she does not have. The son could take no more. As he struck the officer, the mother screamed in horror. Her son had struck a representative of the king. My grandfather makes it clear to his son that nobody is there to witness a spectacle. Such a sight made them feel sad for weeks afterwards. They are there so that one of their own would not be alone in his suffering as his body writhes with each barbaric blow against the noble expression of a son's love. Blows which have the energy of hate behind them. Relentless enough to expose bone. Only when the now almost dead body hangs limply does the sound of the awful blows finally and suddenly stop. My father then aged fourteen would never forget that day. He swears by God that his own sons yet to be born will not forget what he had witnessed - and Nellie - I will not be forgetting what was described to me. One more thing. I do not hate any nationality. It is the mad side of human nature that I hate. Circumstance can draw brutality to the surface from within an otherwise normal man. One hate feeds off the other to create the mix of an occupying army developing a hatred for the people as a reaction to the hate being levelled at the occupiers." [see N15]

The Maddens are crossing the mountain range known as The Great Dividing Range. Almost the distance from London to Jerusalem in length, they can cross at a place where it is about fifty miles wide. As slow-moving bullocks can only be manoeuvred around where the road is wide enough, it can take up to an hour just to move a mile.

As getting to the next inn could be after sundown on a howling winter's night to see the distant lights would be more than just a welcome sight. It would be an enormous relief. It is good that it is autumn. The inn now before us is bathed in a setting sun.

When they settle into the comfort that only a proper building can provide, Nellie reflects on her road experience so far.

"Not once since crossing the Nepean has the threat of bushrangers crossed my mind - yet there was so much talk of them from where we came."

"The poor traveller should not be worried. Bushrangers cannot afford to lose the sympathy the public has for men who have been driven by a pitiless legal system to become outlaws."

Your husband may not be in the right job. In the newly appointed constable's opinion, the law seems to be a weapon of terror.

The horses are almost knocked-up upon arriving at the village of Weatherboard Falls - and it is late enough to call it a day. At dinner the Maddens strike-up with Madge and Sid Finney. Next morning the sign LOOKOUT 2M invites the women to leave Sid and Paddy with the children. Madge's husband warns:

"If the track becomes faint or bifurcates. Turn back. Getting lost could be the end of you."

Not liking the sound of that - but cannot let on to Madge that you are concerned.

It is at the second rest stop that Nellie is getting worried.

"The track is meandering all over the place. That distance on that sign back there may have meant as the crow flies."

"Let us be guided by what Sid's fob-watch tells us. Keep going for another thirty minutes."

It is while engrossed in negotiating the rough surface that they are suddenly jolted into another world by a valley walled-in by almost vertical sandstone cliffs appearing to be two thousand feet high. They sit there at the ledge without speaking - until Madge breaks the silence.

"I am sitting here as if being in a presence of something spiritual and of an age beyond man's knowing." [see N16]

They assume that getting back will be no problem, until coming to a bifurcation in the track which had not been noticed before. Then it came in from behind - now it is clearly there in front. While following the track on the right, Nellie becomes aware of her heart's beating.

"How long to keep going before we return to take the one on the left?"

"But Nellie. What if we turn back - and this is the right track? We will lose a lot of time. Maybe a dangerous amount."

It is when coming upon an odd-shaped rock remembered as having been passed before that Madge exclaims:

"The Lord be praised!"

To this Nellie breathes out:

"Amen to that."

Upon losing elevation, both grassland and sky open before the Maddens.

Behind has been day after day of being rocked and jarred over a heavily broken surface along a road that was either winding or undulating. You have not experienced such motion since the voyage out here under sail - yet maybe you will remember this as an adventure. The novelty of this country affects the immigrant's mind as nothing else he or she has experienced before. Back home change seems to frighten people. Here we accept it with barely a concern - then we rapidly adapt to it. [see N17]

As the Maddens move further onto the plains, what they are experiencing is starkly different to the Illawarra environment.

You had been told that weeks can pass without rain. This you can now believe. The air feels dry. The water in the creeks seems to be barely flowing. There seems to be no moisture in the ground - yet crops grow.

The road into Bathurst is a very welcome improvement on what they had been experiencing. Less climbing, less descending and a much better surface. After that, it is Bathurst to Orange in a cart converted into a coach by boards nailed on top of stumps under a canvas roof. Next day, it is another so-called 'coach' to Molong. When getting close to the town, Nellie is feeling an apprehension rising within her.

You cannot get off the mind the bit about the police being of a lower moral standard than the men they arrest. Your husband will be stepping into an environment in which a uniformed man of the crown is guilty until proven innocent.

MOLONG

After just two days following their introduction to Chief Constable John Davis, the picture is becoming very clear. The officious chief constable stays mostly in his command post where he selects on whim what is to be ignored and selects on whim what is to be nit-picked over. When Davis does leave his comfortable hole, he leaves as a man of such importance that he is seen to almost swagger about the town. Then there are the two mounted men who could be gone for days at a time.

Here in Molong, there is one chief constable, two mounties and one lowly foot-constable. It is clear who will be dealing with the drunks. Even so - you feel proud when you realise that the women of the town are glad of your husband's presence. They do not want their children to witness such degradation - and one never knows what a drunk is going to do next. [see N18]

In May 1857 the third daughter arrives. She is named Ellen after her mother.

There must be some form of contraception. Your bed in another room is the way to go - and not to simply avoid pregnancy. There is no pleasure at all in physical intercourse. The love affair of sorts with the sun on that beach back in the Peabody days has gone as your single life has gone. Most would say that a love affair with the sun could be seen as a bit unnatural. It follows from this reasoning that the grubby marital act similar to what the pigs were doing was natural. Although you are aware that a physical intercourse problem in a marriage can easily widen to become a general relationship problem, you are confident that with the Maddens there will be no such problem. Hardly a day goes by when Paddy does not say to his wife that he loves her - you always responding with the same words for him. Why do you think this exchange occurs almost daily? Maybe embedded at the back of your mind is that this is the man who gave you children - when for all you know nobody else in existence was willing to do that? Maybe at the back of his mind is that you are the woman who rescued him from life-long bachelorhood - when for all he knows nobody else in existence was willing to do that? Maybe it has simply been the passing of time since our marriage and the children born of that marriage that has brought us so close?

Paddy's job is to follow orders with judgments of his own kept to a minimum. There are ex-convicts on tickets-of-leave required by law to attend their respective religious service on Sunday. Paddy ensures that they do. He serves warrants and subpoenas. He maintains the lockup and the men in it. What the law has to say about the operation of a public house he must be well acquainted with - and that being especially true when dealing with one loud-mouthed publican by the name of Jim Mortal.

"In the company of others - and me within earshot - this man Mortal will make remarks about the 'micky constable'."

"This could be a plan to make it difficult for you to report some real illegality without appearing to be seeking revenge. I suggest that you arrest drunks causing problems well away from Mortal's hotel."

"I have been doing that already. Such a damn shame. A friendly town with just this one person there to spoil things."

Since arrival the flagpole on the front grassed area of the station had been bare until the day Paddy hoists the flag of the kingdom before the eyes of his irate wife.

"What is so special about today for that rag to fly on high?"

"The fifth of November. The day when a Catholic attempt to blow up Westminster was foiled. Now I ask: why was that in God's grand plan?"

"Maybe God is not in favour of people being blown-up? Whatever, we both must keep our thinking objective if you are not to lose your job and the accommodation which comes with it. So, high will fly whatever flags are so instructed on whatever days are so instructed."

The only proper church is Wesleyan. All other congregations conduct their Sunday services in whatever building is suitable. It is in Molong that Nellie introduces a religious tradition from home at that time called Advent occurring four Sundays before Christmas

Mesmerising are the four lit candles mounted upon a wreath of leaves left to flicker in a dark room after all other flames have been extinguished. They seem to be reminding you that when you left Kilkenny, you left part of your heart back there.

Then there are the forty days of Lent and light eating leading up to Easter.

Glorious and sacred Easter! Days when your faith seems to almost grab your being and a time to feel good about the world.

Attempting to focus on the good in this world is natural behaviour - but waiting in the shadows is behaviour that is far removed from the good. A constable has no option but to accept the reality as objectively as he can. However, there was no such option available following a crime of the basest kind that occurred when the Maddens are close to leaving Molong. After a Dick Phillips reported a body on his property one of the mounted constables rode back with him to where lay the lifeless remains of an aboriginal female of about fifteen years. Appearing to have been dead for two days, her hands are bound behind her back with fence wire, her head is horribly battered and there are ripping wounds across her stomach and back. Then there was for the two witnesses the alarming sight of an empty bottle jammed in her rear end. Dick had seen no suspicious characters in his area - but his neighbour's wife had. It was five days previously at a time her husband was fencing well out of sight of the house that she sees from a front window a man approaching the door as she catches a glimpse of another moving around to the back as if to check that she is alone. She opens the door to the man standing there. With a carbine barrel pointing at his gut, he says nothing before turning around to call out to his mate. Only after the woman watches them proceed along the road until out of sight can she relax. It was a heinous mutilation and murder on the Phillips' property that was not to leave Nellie's mind.

"The murdered girl's people would have been frantic when they discovered that she was missing. I suspect the two who knocked on Dick's neighbour's door."

"They were on foot. It was not them. The Ophir diggings are where all the district's blacks seem to have moved where they exchange their labours around the digs for white man's tucker of flour and sugar. Ophir is a two-day cross-country ride from Dick's place. The blacks do not find her because she is spirited away by horse. I suspect that the men who could have prevented the snatch were drunk. It does not take much alcohol to send a black brain stupid."

"Nothing remains unknown to God. There can be no escaping of Hell for them."

"So, where is Hell Nellie - and what is it?"

"While St. Mathew refers to a fiery furnace, a priest told me that the torment is not due to actual flames. It was due to the feeling of permanent loss of God. A banishment to a totally empty existence."

"All nonsense. On what authority has the priest to make a statement of fact that is not in the Bible? - and I would like someone to explain to me why missing a single Sunday mass warrants the same eternal banishment to a totally empty existence as does the torturing of a girl for maybe two days - and another thing - upon the loss of my younger brother I felt stressed in the chest and throat for days. The suffering was not in the mind. It was in the body. So, how is a soul free of a body able to suffer?"

When will you learn to not fall so blindly into a discussion about a religious interpretation?

That time for the Maddens in Molong was generally one of contentment - but a lowly man's contentment is of no consequence in this game played by men in high places.

When the queen's poet said that 'ours is not to reason why', he was referring to military men. The problem is wider than that. It seems that once in any uniform, a man becomes less of an individual and more of an unreasoning pawn on a chess board. Now we must move back from the direction we came.

BATHURST

The discomfort in the journey from Molong is being made worse by an awareness that Bathurst has six thousand residents. At the end of the first day, the Maddens are camping in Orange where the driver provides the tent and stretchers. The next night is a stay in the village of Guyong. After tents are pitched in a paddock next to the inn, the driver joins the drinkers where he and they become rowdier by the hour. When the family gets into Bathurst in the afternoon of the next day, their first action is to report to the police barracks where they learn that they will be living with five foot-constables and a sergeant. Next morning man and wife are feeling glum.

Now we know how unhomely this home for this family of five is going to be.

As they walk around on this first full day, they are even noticing change since passing through on the way out to Molong.

There seems to be an energy which is changing the whole colony. Gold fever they call it. Men can behave irrationally and violently when in its grip. Your man's pay fairly covers the dealing with drunks - not for putting his body in front of a gun.

However, Paddy does have to put his body in front of the notorious police magistrate Dr. Palmer. When the great man arrives to inspect the station and to meet any new personnel, he and the sergeant walk into the sergeant's little office without any acknowledgment of the seated man with hands sweating, thigh muscles wobbling and lungs gulping for air. After some minutes the sergeant emerges.

"Constable Madden."

The bark seems to cause Paddy's chest to go into a spasm. He steps through the door to stand two yards in front of the magistrate who continues writing without raising eyes from paper. When he does face the constable, Paddy is about to smile. Palmer's glare kills that inclination.

"Your record at Molong is generally satisfactory - except that just prior to your leaving a James Mortal lodged a complaint with the Chief Justice who mailed it onto me."

While feeling that he is about to faint, the foot-constable in an unsteady voice asks the nature of the complaint. What he hears unnerves him even more.

"You intimidated the hotel's patrons. Even smelling their breaths. Leave the smelling of a man's breath to his wife. Your duties are confined to arresting men causing a disturbance. I am aware that there will inevitably be a few bullies in the force. I do not like them. You are now on notice."

As Palmer is speaking, Paddy is feeling that it is he who is being bullied. That night he is looking at his sleeping children as would a father fearing for their futures.

"I can only remember the one incident when I did not demand to smell the man's breath. I simply said to a man who could not climb into his dray that I could smell his. I am sure that today I sounded exhausted. If my fear was obvious, Palmer would have identified me as being a man of little substance."

This is not what this wife wants to hear. Palmer's aggression could be an indication that he is looking for an opportunity to drive this family's breadwinner out - and this man of yours seems to be very different to most in that he can frankly admit to the emotional turmoil he goes through. One admission you cannot forget was of him being a coward and of your attempt to assure him that he was not. What we call bravery is often due to rage causing one's sense of danger to momentarily vanish. To still stand one's ground when frightened is true bravery.

In bed at the end of the day of the bullying, the wife cuddles into her deflated husband. In the morning a concerned inner-voice is asking:

"Will there be a price to be paid for what happened last night?"

As an addition that further adds to the nostalgia for the house in Molong, in the July of 1858 a daughter arrives. The mother leaves the naming of this fourth child to be accommodated at the barracks to the father.

"Why not the name of the saint who is supposed to be sprinkling stardust over us?"

In the year that follows, Catherine continues to develop without any complications. So, her parents could not understand the reason for what occurred on October 20, 1859. One of the constables at the barracks gave it a name.

"Looks like whooping cough to me."

The sound of the child struggling for air distresses her parents as nothing ever has. It is by the time the doctor finally arrives that Catherine has ceased breathing. As the doctor takes her hand in his, Nellie can hardly believe the words she is hearing.

"I'm sorry. She has gone."

After she attends mass on the following morning, the emptying of the church has left Nellie sitting alone staring at the tabernacle. Fr. Keating - who is to officiate at the burial - is reading at the side of the altar - and it is from there that he notices the grieving mother. Upon leaving his seat he sits beside her.

"Our Lord moves in mysterious ways. It has been his decision. We must not question his decisions."

"I know that father - yet at a time such as this I am angry. I have been thinking of a woman back home who did not lose one of her ten children. To add more power to her prayers, boots beyond repair were secreted away in a cavity somewhere in the house known only to her. When I mentioned this odd practice in one of my conversations with a shipmate, she said that the hidden old boots had no effect on the outcome as it is by the Law of Probabilities that someone somewhere will not lose one child. I thought at the time what Eliza really was saying about probabilities determining outcomes. She was saying that praying is as much of a waste of time as what hiding old boots was."

"Be careful Mrs. Madden. Reject all those temptations to stray from the path to Heaven. To be alive is to accept the losses with the gains. To be gained will be the children to come."

Johanna arrives in April 1860. This fifth girl joins the family when it is living in a small house on Russell Street which is in the same street as the gaol. [see N19]

You know that it may be wrong to pray that there be no more children. Maybe just as wrong for a wife to move her bed into another room - but if it is, then what is God's plan? From what you know of birds the male pursues and the female chooses. It is sexual gratification which drives his pursuing. It is her need for the security of her offspring which determines her choosing. Would that behaviour be fundamentally different for humans? Once a woman's security needs have been met, she would prefer that his contact with her be limited to affectionate embraces - but that may not be generally true. All you can know is how you feel.

The arrival of Ann in the March of 1862 finally leads to a house of their own near the Denison Bridge which spans the Macquarie River. [N 20]

A river course awaiting substantial water to flow in it is typical of the rivers west of the ranges. This is one such river. As the depth of water looks to be about six inches in the middle, a large expanse of dry sand is left for the children of the town play in.

Then there was that week of rain which began less than a month after the Maddens had moved in.

The sight of branches of timber moving by as fast as a man can jog is frightening. If one of the children fell in, it would be the end of her.

While the Maddens are loving the move into the house, Paddy's musing spoils it a little.

"Life has taught me that nothing ever seems to run smoothly for long."

"Since my anger at the loss of our child has subsided, I now agree with Fr. Keating. Whatever happens, good or bad, it is by the will of God that it does."

"God's will be dammed! Your friend Eliza's 'Law of Probabilities' is behind every event. To be alive is to be a player in a great game of chance. From that it follows that to be alive is to be vulnerable to tragedy. We did not lose Catherine because God wanted that outcome. We lost her because we simply were alive to lose her."

Evidence in support of Paddy's nothing-runs-smoothly theory is that a revolver was reported to have disappeared when only he was at the barracks.

"The missing weapon must have been already missing - if there was one missing in the first place. I am afraid that there is to be a fact-finding enquiry in the morning."

It is the next day that Paddy is hearing men talking inside the room and wondering what they are cooking up. After about a ten-minute wait, a sergeant calls him into the room and points to a chair that is directly opposite an inspector. A sub-inspector is seated to the right of him. As Paddy is in the process of sitting down, the inspector asks:

"How's the family?"

This man on the lowest level of police ranking breathes a sigh of relief as what lies ahead may not be as bad as he is fearing it to be. He was wrong. The low talking in the room was the setting up of a trap - and it is the structure of this trap that the questions be friendly at first before incrementally becoming more hostile - to finally being directed at the target's general commitment to his job. In a type of relay, while one man is questioning the target the other is calmly preparing his assault. With this relay-type process occurring on one side of the table, there is no relief for the mounting tension in this lone man on the other side who was recruited at a time when there was an urgency to rapidly build up the numbers of police by raising the age limit and making the applicant's background history less demanding. Having not broken any of the rules he now must be pushed out by men who have experience in attacking those who have no experience in defending. At home he informs his wife of the harrowing event.

"I suspect Paddy that the hatchet-men's initial pleasantry was a tactic to get you to drop your guard and to encourage you into talking freely as if there was no trap being plotted before being called in. I further suspect that the inquiry had nothing to do with any revolver. It was designed to push your tension up to a threshold beyond which you lose control of your tongue. That would be all they need to have you dismissed for insubordination."

You were once informed that feeding an unwanted employee enough rope to hang himself is a well-used management procedure. Anyway, he survived when he could have just as easily not survived. You need to find some way of putting a few more pounds in the bank.

As the sharing of the night duty enables Paddy to be at home for four nights, an opportunity opens for Nellie to earn a few shillings on the gaol's payroll as kitchen hand for two hours in the evening. To avoid all eye-to-eye contact with the prisoner, the staff are to focus on the bowl being ladled into. This Nellie manages to do - except on this one occasion when what she sees goes straight into her heart - and she knew who this person was. One of Peg's childhood experiences was the witnessing of her younger brother receiving beating after beating from the father until the last was enough to put an end to the child's existence. Although the father seems to have left Peg be - the mother did not.

A face with a destroyed eye is difficult to look at. Maybe a pretty face before a demented mother threw boiling milk into it.

Paddy has something to say about this.

"Against a defenceless child our society allowed this crime to be committed by known abusers. From such abuse her antisocial behaviour as a young adult is inevitable. Now we punish the young adult for behaviour for which society and not she is responsible."

On a rare occasion your uneducated husband reveals himself to have a sage's wisdom.

Prior to the Maddens leaving the town, Peg is released and there is the last hanging outside the wall of the gaol.

You cannot help but assume that the poor girl is now in some wretched place where she is barely surviving. You do not want to think of what some men living rough might be doing to her. The good news is that there is to be no more public displays of the killing of a human. With that step forward, the next is to recognise that the environment of the prisons brutalises most of the prisoners and some of the guards. Wherever a prisoner is totally at the mercy of his overseers, the public must realise that abuse hidden from public view becomes inevitable. All assurances that it does not happen must be dismissed.

GUYONG

As Nellie was pregnant with Phillip when they left Bathurst, it is in September 1863 that he becomes the first to be born in the village of Guyong. Zoned as residential for the families of men working the gold mines at Lucknow and Byng, the village is a cluster of about fifty houses in three streets - with another fifty or so are scattered over larger allotments. There is an Anglican church, a post office, a general store, a schoolhouse with a resident teacher in an attached dwelling and an inn. [see N21] About twenty Catholic women take it in turns to host Evening Devotions in their own residence - but not at the Maddens. Paddy states his position on this matter.

"No gaggle of geese squawking god-words on government property."

With his supervisor stationed in Bathurst, it is when Bridget arrives in the November of 1867 that Paddy has established a social status that he has never experienced.

Every struggling family deserves a beam of sunshine breaking through the clouds. Guyong has become this struggling family's beam of sunshine.

However, a sunny sky must cloud over sometime. This it did on May 19, 1870 when his service is terminated with a gratuity of £126.

Aged only 54. A sad day for both man and wife. That highly visible statement that he is somebody in the community is to be worn no more. Although proud as he was to wear it, in Molong and in Bathurst, his were the most demeaning of jobs. If from a low class a man is rarely able to rise above it.

Nevertheless, he submits a written request that he be permitted to keep the brass letter H as a family heirloom.

The refusal of such a minor request when there was probably a drawerful of brass badges held at headquarters is as hurtful for you as it is for him. [see N22]

As Guyong has become a place Paddy and Nellie feel no inclination to leave, they find a liveable two-bedroom house at the edge of town for a very small rent - and it is in August 1870 that Patrick David arrives. With one Patrick already in the family - he becomes David.

The ninth human has been created in your body. Although a man never experiences this satisfaction, at age forty you are feeling that you have had as much creativity as you want.

Within the month the bed of the head of the family is in the shed leaving wife and children the two bedrooms.

Not comfortable with the arrangement. Thankfully, the children are asking no questions.

At the time David is born, the twins are old enough to need a wider circle of young friends. The options are to move west to Orange or east to Bathurst.

It must be Orange. Bathurst holds too many bad memories.

In her notebook, Nellie expresses her last impression of leaving Guyong in a little poem.

The late afternoon of the last day.
The storm is moving away to the east.
Away in that dark sky is a distant rumble of thunder.
To the west the pink is clear to the horizon.
Clean to breathe is the air the storm has left behind.
An aroma is rising from the wet earth.
No perfume could smell as good.
But the fading light is saying:
"Time to get the stove going."

It is on this last night that Nellie reflects on the characters that are as diverse in a community of the size of Guyong as anywhere.

There was Eadie Flynn. A big woman who seemed to have some blood of the South Seas in her. Her only child looked to be aged about nine. Husband Jack worked in a mine in the Byng area. Such a thin man. When you first met him, he looks as if he is dying. A year later, he is still looking exactly as before. So, he could not have been. There was that day when our paths crossed. With daughter Marion clinging to his side, you saw love there - and so respectful of women was that man as he held his hat over his chest all through his conversation with you. Then there was that night of screaming. So upsetting to hear that you cried. You were thinking then that Jack must do something if Marion is not to eventually turn against her father for not protecting her. As it turned out, he was not to be around for that day of reckoning. You could never forget the day. On the ground are what looked to be pyjamas that had blown off Eadie's line. Remembering your mother's advice that a good deed for a nasty person enhances the worth of the giver, as you moved over to peg them back on the line you see that there was a man in them. It was Jack. There was blood all around his head. You hurried back to the house to rouse your husband. Now from the kitchen window you watched him quickly inspect the body and slowly walk back to the house. When he steps into the kitchen, he looks into your anxious face. Throat cut from ear to ear - says he. The bitch - says he. To this you say that it was not the bitch who wielded the razor and that Jack died because he despised himself. When Paddy informed Eadie that her husband was dead in the backyard, except to look startled she showed no emotion. After offering to take Marion, it is when Paddy brings the child to you that you tell the poor little thing that her daddy has been taken to hospital. The girl stays with us that night. It was after the burial on the following day that Eadie collected her daughter. On the day following that there is nobody in the Flynn yard. As no light was seen in the house at any time during the night, it seemed that Marion and her mother have simply walked away. A sombre Paddy had the last say in the matter. You will not be forgetting the words. We are a society which fails its children - says he. For this it must be an outright failure regardless of any of its achievements - says he. Maybe one day only those capable of being good parents can become one by law - says he. Now I am thinking that we should have such a law. Then there was 'Chubby Bar' Bromley the owner of the general store. Nobody seemed to know what Bromley's first name was. His wife even called him Chub - but you do find out how he got the name. The story was that Bromley obtained a large crate of 'Chubby Bar' soap at no cost. Old Bromley asks every entry into the shop to buy a bar of it. He keeps this up for over a year with hardly a sale. Always the same figure shuffling along in his slipper-shod feet, suspenders holding trousers up almost to breastbone and an unbuttoned shirt revealing a yellowish singlet underneath. Through a mouth in his bloated face, he moaned at you. The unfortunate lady this creature was attached to was as sharp as a pin. Thelma was always in conversation with somebody. There was probably nothing happening in Guyong that she was unaware of. When you said to Paddy that to any wife of a foot-constable the working life of a shopkeeper would look appealing - displaying and handling all that stuff. Maybe the man did not like you describing yourself as the wife of a mere foot-constable. So, he informs you that a constant source of stress for any small shopkeeper is the customer asking for credit. Which sounds a right-enough reason not to envy shop-keepers. Now you remember that there was another problem. On the veranda Thelma had set up a table with four chairs and a notice: HOT TEA AND A BISCUIT FOR THRUPPENCE. She was hoping to get her female customers to chat with themselves rather than talking to her as if she had nothing else to do. So, the other problem is that *by being a fixture in a room that anybody can walk into, the shop owner lacks the privacy you enjoy for hours at a time. Then there was 'Old Mouldy' Harrison who Paddy liked to call on for a cuppa and chat. The man had a son Dinny who had been in terrible pain for weeks. Although once he was a bit overweight, he was skin on bones when Paddy finds the old man in a daze and the son laid out on his back with wrists tied together, ankles tied together, a tie binding his jaw with the top of his head and a penny resting over each eyelid. Smothered my own son with his pillow I did - says Old Mouldy. Paddy stared down at the formally laid-out body before turning to the man to look him squarely in the eyes. Keep your silly trap shut because you did nothing of the sort - says he. Old Mouldy did keep his trap shut. Only after Old Mouldy had died himself did you learn that the district copper had covered up a murder. This sad event set you to thinking that after years of believing such a killing to be wrong, you should be willing to concede that it should not be wrong. Old Mouldy was not thinking of an afterlife when all he could be sure of was that his son was in great pain in this life. It was a pain that the father had the means to end. If the church does not regard an execution as a mortal sin, does not regard the killing in a nation's defence as a mortal sin, does not regard the killing in self-defence as a mortal sin - maybe a killing motivated by love should also not be a mortal sin?*

ORANGE

With Guyong behind them, the first house the Maddens have ever owned is in need a lot of fixing.

While not much to look at, 66 Moulder Street Orange is the best place in the world for you to be - and it is to a certain native of Limerick that Orange must also be the best place to be. James Dalton's house 'Duntryleague' is on three levels.

"Paddy. I have been told that the interior of the Dalton house is crafted with disregard for expense as would be expected in a major church."

"Not being a church does not mean that it is not a shrine to a mere mortal who believes himself to be worthy of such grandeur before he has even passed on. More than a home for a common merchant. It is a horn sending out a message to the district that it be known that the man who resides in this place is a man of substance."

When Phillip's mate Michael Dalton shows him through the family home, it is not the ostentation that the Madden boy sees. What he does see has simply fixed a perception in his mind that his father is a total failure.

For a man who has worked hard and honestly to be held in contempt by his own child - you could not be more disappointed for him.

It is by the age of fifteen that Phillip is barely communicating with his father. Desperate to break down the invisible wall, it is on the boy's sixteenth birthday that his father buys him a hat with money he should have spent on replacing his own battered apparel. As he hands the gift to Phillip, the boy stares at it as his parents' hearts are sinking. It is without saying a word that he goes into his bedroom to emerge some minutes later with a bag to walk straight out the front door.

We may be seeing. We are hardly believing.

Paddy says nothing all day until the last of the fire is flickering out.

"It is at the end of a life that the measure of its worth can only be made on a tally of the positive effects it has had on other people. If Phillip does not discover this truth, his life will be of no value." [see N23]

It was a sad mother who retired to bed that night.

We still have our second boy. Even at the age of fourteen, he has a valued position in the tailors' room of R.T. Hawke's. So, his parents always know where to find him - but I have given birth to two sons and always want to have two. Please God. Send Phillip back to us.

In the early years in Orange, the first of Nellie's neighbours she gets to know is Bun Nolan. Although Bernadette was her name, everybody called her Bun. A bit like a pig's snout was her nose and her eyes appeared to be deep-set as they always seemed to be in shadow. At one time, when she and Nellie are conversing, Bun suddenly lowers her voice.

"That woman. The one in that house over there. She had a baby. Born dead it was. But not a human head did it have. It was a serpent's head."

There is a lot of old Ireland still in Bun.

With one of her girls on the keys of Bun's upright, standing on each side is a father and his son.

"Shoulders back boy. Plenty of air in the lungs."

Then begins the Madden rendition of 'Rose of Tralee' with 'I Dreamt I Dwelt in Marble Halls' to follow.

To hear the bonding of father and son through song is sweet to the ear of this wife and mother. There are the songs and there are the stories of the struggles of our people against the intruder

- but it has only been to the boys. That is the way it is in this world. Girls are to be both loved and mostly ignored by their fathers.

Many men travel as far north as Queensland to work both cattle and sheep where they could be away for as long as three months. One such person is Teddy Nolan.

This breadwinner seems to forget at times that he has a family which is going to need actual money to buy bread - yet there is always a Good Samaritan somewhere around. With nothing arriving in the post week after week - it is good thing for the Nolans that there is.

After the difficulty in getting them out of bed in the morning, it is no easier getting the four Nolan girls motivated to do much of anything. The monthly dance for singles brings them to life - and it is through this event that all four eventually find a man. Their mother is far from pleased with the outcome.

"None turning out to be any better than a problem."

The daughters eventually move mostly out of Bun's life - not her two sons. What was once a bonny babe in Bun's arms, she now must witness almost every evening his staggering home followed by his stumbling and his mumbling until he is in his room. However, despite a reputation of going off to the pub at about two o'clock in the afternoon, it is due to demand exceeding the supply of plasterers that Ned is never out of work. At one time Nellie says to Bun:

"Your Ned is a tall and impressive looking man. Your Will is actually handsome."

The mother seemed to glow a little as she heard that. Which is good - because Will has a problem even worse than the demon drink.

When making this assessment of Will to Millie, the brightest of Bun's girls has a warning.

"You had better be careful there Nellie. Some might think that 'worse-than-the-demon-drink' means Oscar Wilde's problem."

"Who is Oscar Wilde? What is his problem?"

"You best ask someone else to enlighten you there."

It seems that Will's 'worse-than-the-demon-drink' problem can be traced back to when Ned hit him over the head with a brick. From then on, the boy complained of headaches until he left school at the age of fourteen. With the passing of the years, Will gradually withdrew into himself to pass most of the day lying in bed. When he did walk about the yard, it was with hands in pockets, an index finger in each ear, boot laces untied and humming what sounded like a Gregorian chant. He could only secure an odd job in the picking and bagging of peas. He rarely went into the town proper and never made a friend. Besides his inability to relate to society, Nellie learns of another strangeness. He would hand her a dictionary with a challenge:

"Pick out a word. Any word."

Whatever word you select he responds with its meaning exactly as it is stated in the dictionary. Thousands of entries in the dictionary - yet his mind has photographed everyone.

In Nellie's later visits to Bun, her strange son had replaced that request with a question.

"What do you understand the word 'sane' to mean?"

Bun informs her that the same question is put to all her visitors.

Of course, this mother will not take the next step and accept that insane is what her son is.

A farmer talks Will into looking after his pigs which are penned five miles out of town. Not to be forgotten is the day the farmer collected Will as it is on that day that Bun sees her son for the last time - his bidding her goodbye was without giving her a backward glance. The mother receives one letter about three months later.

In it is a £1 banknote with an 'All's well' written on a scrap of paper. From then there is to be no knowledge of him until a policeman appears at his mother's door bearing the news that her son's body was found in the creek that passes through his employer's property. Wearing only an undershirt, he had died the previous night when the temperature was below zero.

So, a pointless and probably tormented life has been brought to a timely end by a heart attack.

It was only eight months afterwards that Ned fell off his bike in a drunken state. There was only one rock in one hundred yards for his head to hit. His head hit it.

At funerals the mourners are supposed to mourn. At Will's you did - but not here at Ned's when you are glad that in that box is a problem that is now out of a good woman's life.

When back from the church, Nellie's inner-voice is asking:

"Whose funeral will be next?"

When Paddy insists on painting the front of the house, it is such a hit-and-miss job that his wife is wondering:

Is this the first sign of a failing mind?

As the months pass, he becomes unable to dress himself - always he puts his arm through the neck of a jacket as he can never find the sleeve. Often during the night, he cries out for his parents. At odd times during the day, he will see people in the house who are not there. As his wife must position him on the toilet seat, it was inevitable that she would get him on - but not off. Nellie expected Paddy to be embarrassed when a neighbour must help. The neighbour explains the reason he is not.

"What worries a normal mind does not worry a failing mind."

A nurse from the hospital comes each week in his final month when he is being spoon-fed and his whole body washed. The nurse makes Nellie feel that she is not alone with the problem. She also clarifies the situation.

"Paddy is senile. His mind is slipping away from his brain."

It is when unresponsive for a week, that Paddy suddenly sits up.

"Have you heard from Phillip?"

Is he on the way back - or is the sudden alertness just one of those unusual events in the working of the mind?

They are his last words. As the day of Paddy's parting draws near, his eyes are closed and his mouth partially open. The nurse advises:

"He is losing the ability to swallow. As there is a danger of fluid going into the lung, do not feed him any fluid. His brain is shutting down. You can place a wet cloth on his lips. Our first purposeful action after birth is to suck. When the mind has almost gone it is the last action the body is capable of."

"I hate to think that he has a raging thirst."

"Not to worry. Paddy has lost the capacity to suffer."

The sucking on a wet cloth placed on his lips, Nellie remembers to be his last bodily action. It is when the towel pinned around him is showing no excrement, that the nurse warns:

"Your husband is now only a day or so from passing on to his maker."

It was a small funeral. New arrivals to a town who are already old when they arrive do not make many friends. When she returns to the house, Nellie sits at the kitchen table to contemplate. It is in her contemplation that she reads her poem about the sacred tree written long ago. [see N24]

How you thought back then before responsibilities as a wife and mother gradually reshaped your mind into a more conventional mind. Comforting as it is, you do wonder about your religion. Is there an alternative way to find God? Could you have stepped onto that path when your mind was young and open to change down there in the Illawarra? You thought then that the sacred tree had a soul - and when years later Old Mouldy Harrison killed his son to release him from his agony, you believed then that Jesus would have approved. Now with your partner gone, how could you ever accept that such an honest and kind man who did not believe in Hell would be in Hell? While you stand steadfast in the faith, you feel that you must adjust its teaching on those occasions when it seems to be a proper Christian thing to do. Baptism is not a contract to accept all without question. You now understand that - and those who know you as a religious person are assuming that it was your daily visits to St. Josephs that held you up during the last few months of Paddy's life. That they did - but that was not all that sustained you. To share the final struggle of a person one loves deeply is an experience to round-off a life in the best possible way. [see N25]

THE MARY STORY

WINIFRED MEETS MARY

After a draining ten hours on the train, Winifred Condon is standing on the railway platform in Orange where she sees a woman looking at her as if in expectation of a stranger's arrival.

"Would you be David's wife Teresa?"

"That I am - and you would be Winifred. Mum is living up at Towac close by the old school site. My late sister's husband John Cole lives further up the road at The Pinnacle. The hotel across the street is reputed to be reasonable. Terry Hall should be here tomorrow morning about eight. He would be willing to drive that far."

It is eleven o'clock the next day when passenger and driver are at the site of the Towac public school which had closed two years previously. Only one hundred yards further along is a small dwelling clearly built by the bush materials on hand and by the most basic of tools. As the cab's horse is munching on grass at the roadside with the driver standing idly by, Winifred knocks on the front door. Upon hearing nothing, she moves around to the back to see there an old woman talking to her hens. Instantly she is feeling a little sad. When the old woman senses that she is not alone, she turns to look blankly at the stranger.

"Winifred Condon. Your daughter Teresa told me that you had already been advised to expect me and my reason for wanting to talk to you."

"Yes. I have. As I understand it, her husband David discovered that you interviewed his mother Nellie Madden years ago. He likes what you wrote. Found your address with her papers. Now wants you to do the same for me."

It is a relief to hear that - yet with dull eyes set in a wooden face, this woman looks lost.

They walk to the veranda where there is an old rocker chair. When Mary brings out a kitchen chair, Winifred looks across at the driver who indicates that he is happy to remain with the horse.

"I am aware that you had a lengthy discussion about your life with your son-in-law John Cole about two years ago. I am willing to continue up the road to his place."

As if attempting to comprehend the offer, Mary takes about four seconds to respond.

"Do that. I have been a bit confused lately."

As they sip their teas, Winifred is struggling to get any conversation moving. When cups are empty, there is nothing more to say.

"We had best get up to John's if we are to get back to town while there is still some light remaining."

For the picture she planned to take, Winifred was tempted to bring her Kodak film camera. She settled on her cumbersome Voigtlander plate camera for its superior lens.

"Could I take your picture Mary?"

Again, there is about a four-second delay before responding.

"Take it away from the hut."

With that done, passenger and driver climb into the sulky. As they move off, Winifred waves to a sad looking figure.

The dress she is wearing is what women were wearing sixty years ago in the Old Country.

> Aside: That picture taken on January 21, 1915 at Towac is on the cover of this book.

Now into the climb up to The Pinnacle, Terry adds to what little she knows.

"When you see the Cole place you will be asking why any man would have a farm almost on the top of a mountain in a country as big as this - but when demand exceeds supply, no part is off limits - not even the tops of mountains. When you meet John, you will be meeting another small farmer condemned to struggle from dawn to dusk just to support his brood. John lost his wife Eliza some three years ago. Mary was of very limited help to him in looking after fourteen-year-old Sis, [see M1] eleven-year-old Maggie, eight-year-old Tess, five-year-old Jack, four-year-old Izae and two-year-old Mick. I'm glad that someone is putting something down on paper to mark Mary's life. While the well-to-do are having their histories recorded by their families to some extent, the struggling do not seem to be interested."

"Terry. A lot has to do with the image a family has of itself. Contrast this to the aristocracy in England where family portraits adorn every wall. Those people are obsessed with their family's image."

LOUGHGALL

John Richardson knows that he is fortunate to be a linen stamper at a mill that was in the north. The textile industry had mostly collapsed further south - and he needed a wage more than ever as his wife Margaret has just delivered her second child. After losing the argument over their first child Henry's religion, Mary is to be baptised a Catholic. Nevertheless, the Presbyterian father left the mother in no doubt of his earthly concern.

"Here in Loughgall is inter-religious bitterness that is the most intense in the whole of Ireland. As Catholics are losing just about everywhere, we are handicapping the girl with this baptism." [see M2]

It was a benign feeling towards her father's Protestantism that kept Catholicism from totally capturing her mind throughout her early childhood - even to the extent that Mary ceased receiving the sacrament of confession at the age of sixteen. As before receiving communion confession is mandatory, communion was also no longer a part of her life. This worried her mother.

"If you die your soul goes to Purgatory where it is doomed to be for years. Only after its period of punishment has been served, will that soul finally enter Heaven to join the good souls - but if you commit a mortal sin for which you have not sought absolution in the confessional, there is no Purgatory - there is only Hell."

The loving mother's stress can be dated from the day her daughter was kneeling before a small shuttered opening. When slid open, Mary's nostrils are hit by the odour of spirits. Nevertheless, she opens the proceedings with the traditional 'bless me father for I have sinned.' This is followed by confessing to having told two lies to her mother.

"Now no more lies, especially to God. Have you been playing with yourself?" [M3]

Seconds pass as the girl digests the question before rising off her knees to leave without absolution. A younger girl jumps up from her seat to enter the cubicle.

Will he be asking her the same question - or is her body too child-like for him to be interested? You have been told that a priest is your earthly advocate to be listened to as if the creator himself was speaking through him - but do you accept that this man who smells of spirits speaks for the almighty? No! You do not!

While pretending that she was unsure of what he was saying, at home Mary informs on the priest. Her father is angry.

"Girls and women should confess to nuns. To just up and walk out like that without absolution says something of your rebellious nature. You can convert to my church at any time."

That you will not do. He fears for your physical safety. Ma fears for your immortal soul.

When Mary is aged nineteen, danger is hanging over every Catholic household like a dark cloud about to burst.

There must be a better place to live than this. Since Barry Donlevy was kicked to death by a gang of Peek O'Day Boys, you have been saying this.

Those parishioners with personal problems have only the parish priest to turn to for counsel.

Thankfully, the obnoxious Tom Grogan is somewhere well south of Loughall - even rumoured to have been promoted to the purple.

His replacement has no red face, no bushy eyebrows, no smell of spirits about him - and no finger which every adolescent felt to be directly pointing at him or her. It was with the finger that there came the warning:

"Damnation awaits those before this altar who succumb to the sins of the flesh."

Although Jeremiah O'Sullivan's finger does not jab the air before pointing it down at those before him, approaching any priest is an intimidating experience.

Grogan seemed to enjoy a sense of power when a parishioner could not avoid contact with him. Are you confident enough to approach Fr. O'Sullivan? You will not know until you make a move.

When the big day arrived, Mary excuses herself as she is turning her back on her surprised family standing on the steps. Seconds later she is knocking at the entrance to the sacristy as the priest is in the process of pulling his surplice over his head. When he looks her way, she curtsies.

"You're the Richardson girl. The girl with the Protestant father. I am pleased to see you at mass. Have you any problems practicing the faith?"

"My da leaves all in the family to pray when and where we liked. Father. How can I leave Ireland?"

To such a direct question he hesitates for a moment.

"You are saying that you are willing to leave loved ones never to see them again."

Although she had agonised over this reality for weeks, to hear it said so directly has caught Mary's breath - yet the priest does not want to dismiss what has involved a lot of anguish to get this far.

"If you are thinking of England, be very aware that we Irish are not welcome. Too many of us there already - and the reports on the conditions the Irish are living under in New York are horrifying. [see M4] You may have to be prepared to travel further - a lot further. One of my parishioners emigrated to Australia last year. Her mother said that a returning ship brought the glad news that her daughter is physically well and in a position as a house servant in Sydney. Emigration policy is prone to change. I will need to find out about the system as it currently applies."

After a curtsy and a thank-you, there is a rush around to the front of the church where none of the quizzical faces opens its mouth to ask what the disappearance was all about. Then it is all the way home that the word 'Australia' keeps ringing in Mary's ears.

Exciting to hear that word in your head. Frightening to hear that word in your head.

It rains that night. Even though the tiles had been recently repaired, the leak near the foot of her bed is still there. Nevertheless, the drip and the rapid drop in temperature in the room after the fire dies down do not bother this young woman with more than physical comfort on her mind.

Maybe the desire to leave this place is beginning to consume you?

With six days of stress behind her, to the knocking on his open door the priest turns his head. He smiles as he points to the vacant seat.

"Unlike emigrating to America there is a bureaucracy heavily involved with the voyage to Australia - and for a significant time after landing. The process begins with an application to the Colonial Land and Emigration Commissioners in London. With the arrival of the Approval Circular you will know that your application has been successful. After that you will sign a type of indenture that you will put yourself up for hire or begin to pay the full £14 cost of the passage within fourteen days of arrival. I would not be concerned about that. I hear that demand for young female servants in Australia is high - besides, the indenture seems to me to be bluff. If still unemployed after 14 days, the colonial government will have no option but to simply wait for the part-payments to dribble in. However, you cannot avoid the cost of your kit and whatever it takes to get to England in the first place. Now here is what could be a problem. There are so many Irishmen with a good income in prosperous Australia that many emigrants have nominators living in Australia who pay the £14 or part thereof before the emigrant sails. Because of this private assistance, the colony's Assisted Immigration Act could cease to be applicable in two or three years. The sooner you go the better - and a warning. Those nominated have an advantage for it seems that if their medical and age requirements meet the regulations, the commissioners in England must accept them - but without a nominator, you could be rejected on the suspicion that the priest who certified that the information to be true has allowed his sympathy to cloud his judgment. I must say that you would be an exceptional girl if you did go to the other side of the world. Only about one in thirty emigrating from Armagh are willing to take that gamble - and Mary, if you do leave us never leave God. He will not forsake you wherever on this Earth you may be."

For the remainder of that day an inner-voice torments her:

"You have no nominator. You could easily be rejected by the commissioners. Your dream could be blown apart."

On the day before she is to leave, her father and siblings are unusually quiet. Sitting motionless before a small statue of the Virgin is her mother.

Is she is praying for your safety at sea - or is she praying that you will fail the final check in Liverpool and not sail at all?

After a silent meal of oats, there is just a staring into the fire - and it is as she sits there, that Mary is aware of her mother only three feet away sharing this space for the last few hours they could ever do this.

Your desire to press your body against hers is almost overwhelming.

Each time she looks over to her father, he is looking at her - and it is as she is looking at him, that she can still hear in her head his lament when she announced that she would be leaving.

"If a rich man chooses to leave this desperate land, the whole of his immediate family goes with him. The families of those who struggle to survive must accept being ripped apart. Why is this country not a place worth living in? So many of our countrymen have asked the same question. So much to be angry about."

Later that night as she rises to pee in the pot, a faint light is coming through the window.

The dawning of the last day in the Armagh of your birth.

She wraps a shawl around herself and steps outside into a fog which restricts her vision to about a dozen houses in a street that has not changed since she was born in this house. Before creeping back to her bed, she kisses her father's forehead. Although she thought him to be asleep, he takes her hand and squeezes it.

"I have always been proud of my girl."

The daughter pushes a corner of the shawl into her mouth to stifle the croak about to burst out of her throat before moving to the hearth to stoke the ashes of the previous night.

This simple act of stoking ashes is one of the last of your countless experiences in this house of your birth.

With the horses snorting and swishing their tails, it is on a frosty morning that the coach for Portadown Station awaits the passengers. As she hugs her father, Mary feels him take in a deep breath. It is after her weeping siblings hug her in turn, that she comes to her mother.

It is hard to believe that in your arms is the most precious human in your life who in seconds will no longer be there.

Mary boards to join two young men and an older man with his wife who have come in from their nearby farms. As she wishes to sever the link at the instant the wheels begin to roll, Mary has asked the family not to follow the coach down the road. It is while she waits in dread for the driver to cease his chatting, that a small crowd has gathered to see them off. As they finally begin to move, a man calls out:

"Don't forget poor Ireland."

When she looks back to see a figure wrapped in a black shawl, Mary whispers:

"Mummy."

While looking out the window the retreating grass is telling her that with every minute Loughgall is moving further behind the hills - and it is as the distance widens, that which lies ahead is becoming more of a reality in her mind. As she stares blankly at the middle-aged woman sitting opposite, the gloomy words of Kate McCarthy rise from the depths exactly as she said them when Mary had reached the age of sixteen.

"Many more trails ahead Mary. You will be required to draw on your capacity for courage to an extent that only a man in battle will be required to do - by this I mean that you will allow yourself to become pregnant knowing that you could be dead in nine months. Then after suffering the agony of childbirth, your child could just as not survive beyond infancy as to survive it. In your aging you will be crippled by any one of several women's complaints for which there is no cure and barely any treatment. Never will you be at complete ease due to the potential threat of male lust and male violence. It is a burden being a Catholic, terrified by your own priests and lorded over by Protestants - but it is a greater burden being a woman. In your travels you may be able to escape from injustice and want. You cannot ever escape your woman's body."

LIVERPOOL

In Belfast, as the immigrants watch the cargo and stock animals being moved below, they realise that they are to be left fully exposed on deck. That horror was later justified when for a period of almost five hours they endured a freezing storm as they clung to each other in fear of being swept overboard. After thirty hours at sea, they finally tie-up at the Liverpool docks.

Written on the faces of those struggling to move is bewilderment. All must be thinking as you are that this has surely been an experience never to be forgotten.

In the Government Emigration Depot, the assisted immigrants are identified, medically checked and their baggage checked. Then something delightful - a hot meal. Later her ship is pointed out to Mary.

You know what ocean-going sailing ships are supposed to look like - but this ship looking so small and fragile - that is something else again.

By noon the next day all have left the mayhem on the wharf behind and are aboard.

In your fellow passengers' voices is the same excitement edged with fear that you have been feeling since stepping off the unmoving wharf and onto the gently moving deck. Are our bodies destined for the deep before any of us can ever step onto a motionless surface again?

As the demand for the steam tugs on this day exceeds the supply, the alternative requires a light anchor to be connected to the capstan by a rope which is then run out by tender to about three hundred yards. Upon the turn of the tide, the ropes come off the bollards and the men strain on the capstan causing the ship to move away from the wharf and towards the light anchor to await a breeze. When the canvas cracks with the first gust and the anchor is quickly weighed, Mary hears a cry that seems to send a jolt through to her bone marrow.

"We're off!"

When the figures on the wharf are out of sight, all move down into the dimness below following a call to clear the deck. Except to ask the person closest for a bit more room down, not much is said by anyone. Mary had already stowed her kit in the hold when she hangs her immediate needs above her bunk in the canvas bag supplied by the Government Emigration Depot. It is as she lay on her allocated space that the image emerging in her mind of her family watching the coach move away triggers a tightness inside her chest and in her throat.

The excitement you felt when the embarkation order came now seems to have become an event in the life of a different person.

She lay in her bunk with her miserable thoughts as she waits for the hours to pass until the lighting of the lamps becomes the one lasting image of the most momentous two days in her life.

How could anybody turn her back on her family as if they had just been put in a hole in the ground, covered with earth and a cross stuck on top? God help you.

SYDNEY

Whenever the hatch is opened the suddenness of the morning light is the most welcoming experience at the end of every long night - and it is on this day that what the voice coming from above is saying is far more welcome than on any day so far.

"Ladies. The coast of New South Wales. Now portside."

By day we had visions of the place, by night we had dreams of the place - and now the place!

As the ship approaches the gap between the headlands, there are fifty assisted immigrants on top at ten-minute intervals.

The good captain has allowed that many at a time to be on deck for one very good reason. This approach so stirring of the emotions one could not imagine the likes of which would greet any immigrant to any other land on this planet. Moving directly into Sydney harbour through a gap between two headlands is as if we are gliding through a great open gate into a new world. How do you feel? A mixture of relief to have arrived, apprehension of what lay ahead - and a vague feeling of unease as the only people in the world you love are now at the opposite side of the globe from this thrilling sight.

Now down below in the dimness the excited girls can only feel the gentle rolling. Mary puts her hand on her bunk for a last feel of where she had spent many an uncomfortable night.

Another immigrant will be lying here - may even die here.

In the few days spent anchored off the Quarantine Station, the girls do something about cleaning themselves before officialdom steps aboard in the persons of the Colonial Secretary, the Port Health Officer and the Immigration Agent. Hoping for ticks in their performance reports, before these said persons, the surgeon and the matron are standing stiffly. With this process done, the ship moves on to the disembarking. As some nominators may live several days journey from Sydney, delays in the forthcoming money and travelling instructions for those to be in their service must be allowed for. So, a single female can have free lodging on the ship for up to fourteen days. Without a nominator, Mary goes directly to the Hyde Park Depot where she is interviewed by a clerk of the Immigration Board. After that comes what every immigrant had been desiring for months - a hot bath - for which she has the good luck to be second in line. When back into the room of forty or more unwashed bodies, she believes she knows the reason for the sudden stench.

A room smelling of soap must have cleared out your nostrils.

By the second day the filth has been washed off every assisted immigrant.

The girls look thinner and older than what had left England. That was three months of broken sleep ago, three months of gut and stomach problems ago, three months of scratching ago, three months of back pain ago, three months of gasping for fresh air ago - and three months of fear ago.

As these gaunt faces and bony bodies will be on display shortly, Mary overhears matron say to some government man:

"This coming hiring day will be far removed from the Shrewsbury Flower Show."

It is towards the end of the hiring period that about a quarter of the girls remain.

The leftovers look rather battered. That must be what you look like.

As a concern that nobody may wish to hire her is growing into actual stress, a man is standing before her.

"Name's Gary Finch. I'm a solicitor. I live in the suburb of Glebe. It is not far from here."

After signing the agreement, the two walk to the sulky in a silence so uncomfortable that Mary feels that she must say something.

"Sir. What would you like to know about me?"

"Your report stated good health and good behaviour. That is all I wish to know."

The young woman's heart sinks.

This man you may have to associate with for many months seems to have no understanding of how desperate single young immigrants are to be welcomed. All he had to do was ask you something about your voyage.

As she takes her bag down from the sulky, Mary turns to see before her a woman of about her age.

"Sarah Connolly. I will take you to your room."

The first room she has ever had to herself is light and airy. Then reassuring words from Sarah.

"I know how you feel. I was scared on my first day too. Loneliness is the immigrant's overwhelming feeling. Any human willing to be a friend will do."

If Sarah and you could be good friends - and if she could introduce you to her friends, you would not feel to be so alone.

Mary had just unpacked her meagre belongings when Sarah arrives with undergarments and outfit. The dress is black - all else is white.

This dress fits well. The last girl must have been about your size. As Finch knew so little about you, your size could have been the only reason you were hired - but your dilapidated old shoes will need to be replaced.

As Sarah is slipping one of her shoes onto the new arrival's foot to check for size, Mary speaks down to the top of her head.

"Are you happy here?"

Sarah does not look up from the new arrival's foot.

"It will have to do until I find a suitable man. The master of the house would be no problem if he did not look through you as if you do not exist. His wife is a bitch. The children are dreadful."

Now through the open window, Mary is hearing a male voice which seems to be saying that the new biddy has arrived.

"Sarah. Did you hear what I thought I heard?"

"Biddy is the derogatory label for we Irish female imports. In the tiny mind of the chap you have just heard, we have all been named Bridget by mums who were named Bridget and whose own mums were named Bridget."

"If the gardener feels small in himself, he may need to have somebody around that can be put down to compensate for what is out there which puts him down."

"In this place the mistress treats the so-called master of the estate like a dog - but that cannot be due to her feeling small in herself. Just the opposite. She behaves as a queen who throws an occasional slice of cake to the peasants at the gate."

In her room are a pitcher and basin on a stool, a mirrored chest of drawers with a candlestick on it and a bed with a multi-coloured knitted spread on top and a chamber under it. A white curtain covers the window. Mary cleans her face before walking to the top of the wide staircase of polished mahogany.

Everything about a rich man's house is designed to enhance the self-esteem of the owner. There is so much in this world to make a person of your ranking to feel to be of small value as a human.

She takes a deep breath before stepping onto the first step. Now in a large sitting room the lady of the estate has her back to the new hired help. When Mary timidly taps on a sideboard, Roslyn Finch does a half-turn towards her.

"Come here girl. How is your room?"

Before the help can answer, the boss-lady issues her first order.

"You are to assist Sarah in the preparation of dinner. Dining room is through that door. The kitchen attached to that."

Mary thanks her before moving towards the dining room as an inner-voice is scolding:

"Damn! Your 'thankyou madam' had a quiver in it."

When she steps through the door, it is in a whisper that Sarah asks:

"How did it go for you?"

To this Mary whispers:

"The mistress sure has a fierce-looking mouth."

Then more whispering from Sarah.

"That is just the signal to beware of the explosives. When the fuming starts is when you will see on that puss a very large picture of fierceness."

It is still light on this her first day when Sarah offers to show the new girl around the grounds which look to be between a half-acre and one acre. She points to the trees with the most massive trunks.

"Morton Bay Figs. Those with the wide light green leaves - Liquid Ambers. The two sentinels at the gate - Norfolk Island Pines. The four tall ones - Sydney Blue Gums."

It is as they stroll along the paved pathways which meander through plots of flowers, that Mary sees a young man pulling weeds and an elderly man pruning bushes.

"That skinny young fellow would have been the one who referred to me as the new biddy."

Sarah looks squarely into Mary's face.

"Can you read and write?"

"I can still read - but am no longer able to write. After learning to read, I never had occasion to write."

"Then you will always be vulnerable to being referred to as a biddy. Even a ten-year-old here can write - and if you cannot write, you must be a poor reader."

What Sarah is really saying is that you are in a box labelled 'nobody' and that you had best do something about it. [see M5]

Setout at this first dinner involving the new arrival are two tables - the three children to sit at one - Finch, his wife and her sister to sit at the other. It is after dinner when Mary is cleaning up in the kitchen, that Sarah joins her with a report.

"When I heard your name mentioned, I strained my ears to hear what the mistress had to say about you. She said that if you clearly understood who the head of the house is, then any inappropriate advance made by her husband towards you would be stonewalled by you as your fear of the supreme commander would leave no room in your emotions to fear her husband. So, the person who is supposed to be head of the house just sits there and listens to this. How is that for a marriage? Then the ugly sister chipped in to say that her husband once mounted a clandestine rebellion against his marriage vows and that it was a rebellion that was crushed. 'Crushed' is the word she used. She goes on to say that men may be the favourites of the laws they made for themselves - but that a confident woman can make mincemeat out of a man unable to control his weaknesses. Her finishing touch is to declare that to be Natural Law."

"Sarah. Minced man-meat exists only in the fantasies of women who feel superior due to their posh living. One way or another, the two husbands are winning - and that being the real and actual Natural Law."

What you just said to Sarah was clever for a nobody.

When relieved by Sarah every second Sunday, Mary uses the opportunity to get to know a city where energy is seemingly radiating from its citizens as if they visualise a future worth staying alive for.

You have been told that about one-hundred-thousand Europeans live here. It feels that there must be half that number again passing through on the way to the goldfields. Then there is all that construction work at the docks in anticipation of more ships bringing more people and more of the manufactures of England - to return with our wool and gold - but it is the closeness of a natural landscape that makes Sydney dramatically different to Belfast and Liverpool. In every direction is a landscape that seems to have not been altered by man in any way. [see M6 and M7]

It is on one of those Sundays that Mary receives an invitation from a neighbour that she accompanies that woman and four of her female friends on a walk to the big beach in the Bondi Estate. It is upon arrival that she sees a long and wide crescent of golden sand.

There would be many beaches in the world as spectacular as this - but not in a city that might one day hold one million people.

Although privately owned, walking along the water's edge are a few young men with trousers rolled up above the knee. The two young women with them have their drawers pulled above the knee. [see M8]

In white dresses and white wide-brimmed hats, those females sitting on canvas chairs on the beach seem almost to be in a uniform.

It is at the edge between sand and scrub that the six females have lunch sitting on the two table cloths and under the two parasols that the group carried in with them.

Not often can you describe an experience as enjoyable. This one is. One day you just might come back wearing a stylish dress and a wide-brimmed hat - both in brilliant white.

As her days-off were becoming more welcome - her days-on were becoming more dragging. Finally, following a dispute with his wife over a matter of which both Sarah and Mary are completely unaware, Finch puts £1 in his most recent employee's hand as he tells her to go. After Mary finds a two-room place in Pyrmont, she moves into a job in a laundry where five other single women are employed. It is at the end of her first week that she realises what she has gotten herself into.

For women, they are hard drinkers and associate with some rough looking men.

One of her workmates is Stella. One day at knock-off time Stella has an invitation for her.

"You must see some lace that has been in my family for generations."

Although you do not want to, you have no excuse not to - and you must work with this woman.

Upon arrival at Stella's there is an ugly argument two doors down in a street where the manure has not been picked up for days. While not feeling good about the situation she is in, Mary walks directly into Stella's sitting room from the street. As Stella greets her, Mary warns:

"Cannot stay long. Want to get home before dark."

The woman of the house sits her guest down, goes into her bedroom and closes the door. Nine or ten minutes later she emerges wearing an off-the-shoulder blouse and a frilly skirt ending six inches above her ankles as rings dangle from her ears and bangles rattle on her wrists. Her cheeks are rouged and she reeks of perfume.

"What happened to the lace Stella?"

Just then there is a knock on the door. After Stella calls out that the door is open, one of the men moves towards a smiling Stella while the other stands about eight feet away from Mary who is sensing a pair of eyes almost drilling into her chest. As the man with Stella begins to feel her, she giggles. This she instantly stops when her workmate moves towards the door.

"Don't go Mary. You need a bit of fun in your life."

Before the second man blocks her path, Mary shoots past and is out the door. In getting back home she keeps looking back over her shoulder. Finally, when behind a locked door and seated in her rocker, an inner-voice advises:

"You were promised to that man. You do not need to experience that again."

April 8, 1862 is the day the right type of company is about to enter her life. The ANNIE WILSON is berthing with twenty-year-old brother David on board. Also with David is a man who had expressed an interest in Mary before she had thought of emigrating. When she sees her brother waving, her heart seems to miss a beat. Moments later they are falling into each other's arms.

You are hugging home.

As they embrace, the sister is looking over the brother's shoulder while struggling to smile at an uneasy-looking James McGuire.

He looks much older than you remember him to be.

Two or three rests on the way are necessary for the new arrivals' weakened legs to get to her place at Pyrmont. As her financial plight is obvious to her debtors, it is within seconds of getting inside that David has an assurance for his sister.

"James and I are very anxious to find work to repay the deposits made on our behalf."

After dinner, the three reminisce about Loughgall until ready to retire to bedding on the floor which had been loaned in anticipation of their arrival. Now in her own bed, Mary is reviewing the situation so far.

Even if James is feeling uncomfortable due to your obvious lack of interest in him, he has not felt as good for a long time. He may even have given himself a less-than-even chance in a land where males greatly outnumber females.

As the demand for male labour in the colony is insatiable, many male immigrants head inland as soon as they put a few pounds on their bones. Not so for David and James as both almost immediately find work around the waterfront paying £8 a month.

Good in one way and annoying in another. You would have to sweat in a laundry for two months for that. Such is the lot of being an economic unit shaped like a female.

Now a month since the arrival - and a new reality.

Another week with James under the same roof just cannot happen. This awkward politeness must end. What he owes you for his nomination must be written off. You have imported a man who is twice your age from ten-thousand miles away. That never did make any sense.

Following the asking of her brother for the space to speak privately to James, it is after dinner early next evening when all is quiet that David suddenly makes an announcement.

"I feel like an ale with Rooster before the pub closes."

With that announcement, he is out the door.

Rooster sounds to be a bleary-eyed regular leaning up against a bar - yet you cannot criticise David for his choice of friends. Once off the ship, there is a strong urge to make friends with anybody with a friendly face. It is an urge that can result in strange characters becoming so-called friends. James looks a little down that he was not invited. The poor man is now going to be even more disappointed.

Mary takes a deep breath.

"James. I'm not interested in marrying you."

Damn! Those words sounded so cruel.

While expecting him to ask the reason for her nominating him, he simply informs her that he is going for a walk. As soon as David steps through the door, his sister greets him with the news.

"The planned deed is now a done deed."

"I know that the time had to come - yet I feel sad. I have known James a long time. What was your interest in a man twice you age?"

"After asking myself the same question, I arrived at two answers. Firstly, the fact that he was a loyal mate of our father caused me to look at him in a good light. Secondly, in the time I have been in Sydney, I have had two initially promising relationships which ended badly on the second meeting. I suppose under these circumstances, memories of a steady and reliable James became rosier."

It was after leaving the door unlatched that Mary reviews her position.

At fifty, James is so old that his Irish behaviour would never leave him. At age twenty, you were anxious to make a new you when you got here. There was next-to-no possibility that the marriage would survive. Stop feeling so bad about it. You have done the right thing.

As there is no James in the morning, a worried Mary is imagining him lying in a gutter drunk somewhere until David notices that the man's bag is missing. An immense relief surges through his sister as she fully grasps the sudden shift in circumstance.

You simply must accept that James would never have left Ireland if you had not paid his way. That £7 he still owes you could be your contribution to his start of a new life here.

David continues to live with his sister until his debt is fully paid. With that done, he finishes up on the wharves to look for work outside of Sydney. [see M9]

He is almost brimming with excitement. It is as if a golden road is stretching out in front of him. Whatever is wrong with this country, David will not see it. When the desire is to see only good - then only the good will be seen. No perspective in life could be more fruitful to have. So, what then is your perspective? Hasn't there arrived in your God-given life a challenge to put some real work into getting yourself out of the hole lonely people occupy? The unrespectable Stella's introduction to an undesirable man has shown the way. Now through a respectable woman you meet a desirable man. Sarah just may know somebody who knows somebody who knows somebody.

Mary calls into the Glebe house on a Sunday in time to catch Sarah before she gets away to mass.

"There is a seamstress working above a dress shop in George Street. Patsy was once interested in this man before she met one who wears a tie and a starched collar as he balances the books of business. I will ask Patsy to arrange that this fellow and you meet."

"Unlike Patsy I have no dreams of a man in a starched collar. I just want a man I can believe in."

"His name is Patrick McCaffery. He is a driver of an ale cart delivering kegs from the brewery to the waterfront pubs. I would bet £10 that he does not wear a starched collar."

As the man stands before her, Mary's eyes move from the tartan cloth cap, down to the string tie, down to a white shirt under a waistcoat which looks new - finally, to arrive at trousers fraying at the top of his boots.

So far all's good - except that the fob-watch and chain is an obvious attempt to get the man to look to be a bit more than a driver of a brewery cart.

At this 'pleasant Sunday afternoon of tea and biscuit', there are one couple and another single woman. As the one male and Patrick chat, the four women are left to their own chatting. Even though conscious of the carter's presence, Mary chats sensibly enough. After about an hour the single woman leaves - the couple soon after her. Patsy goes upstairs to her bedroom 'for a few minutes.' In the time that it takes for her to return, Patrick's shyness has put Mary at such ease that they agree to meet up on the following Friday. She kisses Patsy and waves the carter a goodbye. On the way home, a surge of energy is flowing through her.

Similar backgrounds mean a kinship in spirit and the best possible start to a marriage. Marriage! You have only conversed with him for twenty minutes. That may be enough. One tooth is looking as if it would need extracting. Fortunately, it is towards the back of the mouth. The next tooth most likely will not be. Getting to know the man as quickly as possible must now be the plan.

It is on that following Friday morning that her waste-no-time plan has put Mary sitting next to Patrick on the cart. Having left the brewery, they are into the cyclic route via eight pubs.

"Patrick. Up here it is exciting hearing the clip-clop of the heavy hooves, seeing the red and white plums dance with their bobbing heads and seeing the metal studs in the leather harness reflecting light like mirrors as those great broad rumps move."

"Clydesdales, Mary. A gift of Scotland to the world."

After three drops, Mary already feels to be completely relaxed in this man's company.

"Although I respect you for doing honest work, I am concerned that this work is an integral part of the biggest social problem we have. It is shameful to see both men and women outside a public house on a Sunday waiting for the doors to open. Then, at the very moment the set period for church services expires, rush in with the desperation of Arabs lost in the desert."

"You should see me as contributing to the betterment of society by distributing ale as a substitute for rum."

Best to not comment on that.

By noon Mary is realising that earning an honest coin can be dangerous as Patrick has to get the kegs to the cellar door where the cellarman takes over.

It is in the getting there that the finger-crushing, toe-crushing and knee-smashing kegs roll as easily as a wheel. That is a worry. One sees so many men with work related permanent injuries.

However, there was one comical moment when they get to one pub just as a customer is being ejected. After landing on his backside in the lane, he raises his hat and waves.

If the fool does not know where he is, there is some unfortunate woman who knows exactly where her dream that turned to disaster is - and you are feeling good in being able to say to yourself that the man at your side is not a fool. Is it nature's pressure to become a mother which causes a single woman to feel the need for a man? Is it the culture which causes her to feel to be an oddity if she does not have a man? It may be neither. It may simply be the single woman's incapacity to prevent a drift into penury.

As the weeks pass, life ticks away steadily until the Saturday when Patrick fails to meet up outside the Terminus Hotel as arranged. Mary is standing at the agreed place when one of the barmen recognises her.

"Your man is in the park opposite."

When she finds him there unable to speak beyond a low mumble, she does not mince her words.

"Your brain is sozzled. Stupid arse."

Next day there is a knock on her door. She opens to see standing there the stupid arse from the park. Now looking into his pleading eyes, Mary is feeling that she needs this person as much as he needs her.

"Patrick. Would you like to move in with me?" [see M10]

ARALUEN

By the time their little boy is finding his feet, the money the family's head can bring in barely equals what is going out.

Stories of lucky strikes have been exciting men for the past sixteen years. Nevertheless, of the grand houses in Sydney where there was bush thirty-odd years ago, it is doubtful if more than a very few were due to gold. Most likely the owners have simply reached out above their level to grab at a passing opportunity. Most of them did not have family wealth, nor education, nor the connections enjoyed by privileged families. So, you know that you cannot be satisfied for long with the work of your man creating husbands who cannot find their way home. Should we be reaching above our level?

Mary's thinking becomes clearer when a letter arrives from David stating that he is averaging £12 a month working for a mining company in the Araluen field. Patrick raises his eyes from the letter.

"Can you think of a reason to object to us earning £12 a month? I can't while the money is out there waiting."

Little Patrick is twelve months old when they arrive at the diggings.

Why are we here? We are here to reach above our level - and that to start with getting out of a tent. The scene here is a hive of activity as great lumps of iron thump for hours a day crushing rock. The leftovers from the crushing called mullock heaps are an eyesore. The earth removed from the stripping process is called the overburden. It is also an eyesore. The trees all gone to fuel the steam engines required to drive the batteries of stampers. This place is depressing. It would not take much of a disappointment for us to clear out - and the father of your son is so much like your own father that from now on you call him Dad. An honour bestowed that has been well earned.

It is after their first dinner that Dad and Mary are looking out over the scene before them.

"This is what the pursuit of money does to the land Mary - especially a mining company's pursuit of money. They know what a mess mining has done to the countryside in Britain - yet the carefree attacking of the earth is repeated here."

"We too will be numbered amongst the attackers. At least we will not be carefree attackers."

"Are you saying that a destroyer with a conscience is more noble than a destroyer without one.?" [see M11]

With six months gone since the McCaffery arrival, the frequency of the floods in the Araluen Valley is pushing several companies to the point of pulling out. At one time there were around ten thousand miners here. In this year of 1868 there are only about three thousand. Even so, there are still many wooden shanties and hundreds of tents pitched in this valley about sixteen miles out of Braidwood - but it is after the passing of those six months that all has not turned out as hoped for the McCafferys.

"My aching back and shoulders would be acceptable if the money was good. No longer is the company money good as more effort must be put into processing enough gold to cover costs. We took a gamble. We must accept the outcome - but even in the glory days before the shafts appeared, a lot of panning and sluicing was required to accumulate enough specs of dust to be the equal of a nugget the size of a walnut - yet nuggets picked up off the ground were part of the mythology of Australia making the rounds in London pubs."

"Speaking of pubs Dad, I have been told that there are twenty-eight of them still here even after so many miners have left. I have also been told that there is a dance hall of sorts with imported girls somewhere up the creek. This I believe. At dusk the scent of lotion is in the air as men pass by in that direction. With so many heading that way, I assume the scruffier ones must be missing out in feeling silk clinging tightly to a female waist. I would hate to be one of those women."

"If they are all like the Stella person you told me about - they would not mind."

Nobody could be more removed from a dancehall girl than a lass brought out to build a new nation with her hands, her back and her womb. As Rosanne Donnelly is to marry Mary's brother in Braidwood's St Bede's church, the happy groom-to-be has some advice to give.

"You and Mary should follow us. Solemnise the union in the eyes of God. If not in his eyes. Then in the eyes of society for your child's sake."

Three months later, Dad and Mary have taken the advice - but not in St. Bede's.

"No need to go any further than the hut-church here at Araluen, Mary. A certificate issued here is as good as one issued in a cathedral - and there are in our little church some fine cedar pews."

"I have no real objection. Expensive looking Catholic churches have always been a worry for me. The cynical Protestants would likely see the fancy St. Bede's in Braidwood as a good luck charm of the superstitious Irish." [see M12]

Cedar pews or not, you would have preferred to not be married in something a little more than a glorified miner's hut.

One of Mary's teeth which had been bothersome for weeks led to an episode in Araluen with a travelling American dentist who introduces himself as Dr. Fromholtz.

"You look anxious Mrs. McCaffery."

"I have an image of my mother with her arms strapped down, her mouth full of blood and evil-looking pliers in the bowl besides her."

"Your mother had no gas. That will not be your problem."

Regardless of what the gas is supposed to do, Mary is frightened as the man takes a needle-like instrument out of a pot of boiling water on a small stove. Seconds later it is inside the patient's mouth. Upon probing from side to side, the slight jump of the body in the chair tells him where he is to attack. He places a cup-like device over her nose before turning a tap on the top of a large iron bottle. A few seconds later he removes the device.

"Get a grip on the armrests."

After the sight of the pliers causes the patient to tighten that grip, the 'doctor' moves the tool back and forth inside her mouth until before her eyes is the offending tooth.

The cussed thing has gone. This Yankee dentist knows what he is doing. Now your stomach does not feel so good.

It is before the year is out that continuing flood damage to so much of the diggings finally forces both the McCafferys and the Richardsons to accept that they will be joining the multitudes of bush nomads. It is when climbing out of the valley that Mary has a flashback to a moment in time when she was complaining to a man that she has had more bad luck than good.

You can see him now. His hand on your shoulder. His face looking into your face. The expression on his is saying that this is a man who knows almost everything. The expression on yours must be saying that before him is a woman who knows almost nothing. Then comes the wisdom. Your every single experience - says he. The good and the bad and the in-between - says he. All have contributed to the making of your unique self - says he. So, what was going on at Araluen that contributed to the making of the unique you? The bad experiences you had been advised to have no regrets about - so, you will not - but something must have surely been going right which in time could make you feel reasonably good about our days in the Araluen valley. What of the many fires becoming increasingly prominent in the fading light? What of the distant sound of harmonicas after most had finished their dinner?

BATHURST

With as many as 1,000 houses here in Bathurst, not much is sold in Sydney which cannot be bought here at a Bathurst price. During the heady days of the gold rush, the number of diggers flooding in could triple prices in days. The McCafferys rent a sizable house on a sizable lot on Durham Street - and by 1874, size is what they need as to Pat, Bernie and Eliza is added David.

It seems that a mind located in substantial surrounding space becomes a spacious mind. In the Old Country a town's streets were narrow. Here they are wide. With so much land, ordinary housing lots fronting town streets are large enough in area to keep a horse.

> Aside. The reader would be wondering why there has been no mention of Bernie and Eliza until now. With no mention in Winifred's notes, and my finding no birth certificates which might state where the family was living at the times the two were born, I could only work back from Bernie's date of death and Eliza's date of death. He was born in 1870 and she in 1872.

Mary accepts without complaint that at the end of the day's work at the local farmers' and graziers' cooperative that Dad does not come straight home.

He needs to have social contact with other men. His favourite 'The Sportsman's Arms' is just one of sixty pubs in the town - yet at the back of your mind is the day you found him drunk. You only took him on after his oath to never abuse alcohol again - which he has so far stuck to - nevertheless, you should have no problem accepting any man who simply holds a glass in his hand as a type of prop as he delivers his baloney to men who are so intent on preparing their own baloney that they are deaf to what he is saying. As you see it, upper-class men are competitive in government and commerce due to the pursuit of power or wealth driving that sense of competition. Lower-class men who are poor and powerless can only compete in bravado and exaggeration. Maybe by enabling that need to be expressed, pubs subdue a man's level of frustration with his lot in life? - and that must be a good thing for the wife.

There is one time when Dad gets into trouble at his watering hole. When he staggers through the front door, his wife is shocked at the sight of blood in his hair, covering his face and over his jacket - all of it coming from a gash about two inches long in his scalp. This Mary cleans and holds a cloth over it until the bleeding stops.

As his ribs are aching from being kicked while he was down, you can thank God that he was not kicked in the head as happened to a man in Pyrmont who never regained consciousness before he died.

The story is that Dad joined a poker game in the pub with five shillings in his pocket. It is with £2/10/- in that pocket that he announces that he has a family waiting. Ignoring the protests, Dad leaves to walk the half-mile of partially-lit lamps. Within five minutes of his leaving, he senses that he is being followed. He quickens his pace. With the sound of running behind him, there is suddenly a figure in front. As he tries to sidestep what is in front, the two behind are already upon him. They hold him while the man in front finds the money in his pocket before whacking his head with some object. After Mary has finished dressing the wound, she is wondering:

Who were those men who had such an emotional stake in the game as to become aggressive? They would have been habitual gamblers who live for the big win. Not the right company for a man who might play less than a dozen times a year to drop into - . and what is it that drives the craving of the gambler? It cannot be greed as the greedy live-in dread of losing their wealth. Is it that a big win enables the little man for a very short time to throw money around as the rich and powerful can do? As Dad walked out the door, they were watching a man denying them a future experience for which they crave. In their minds he had no right to do that.

Since moving to Bathurst, attending mass in its substantial church has become a routine Sunday activity. Even if the sermons are as irrelevant to everyday living as they ever were, Mary has loved since childhood the mysterious and supernatural feel about the dead language of the church. So, the Latin ritual on either side of the droning is more than compensation. It is at one Sunday mass that the priest departed from the droning to make a statement to suddenly snap Mary out of her boredom.

"More of the faith should be sitting in parliament."

Religion should have nothing to do with building a nation. Catholics infiltrating government as church policy could mean that the bishop would determine what the elected member would vote for or against. If non-Catholics suspect that there is a church-led conspiracy to influence law-making, life for us would become very uncomfortable.

It was this sermon which led her to think more than usual of her Durham Street neighbours - the stock-and-station agent Sam Bloom and his music-teaching wife Ruth.

You suspect them to be Jews. They do not attend any church on a Sunday. Keep entirely to themselves on a Saturday. As Jews seem to be clever, there would be very few bush nomads who are Jews. The fact that the stupid revile the clever could explain why the Jews seem to be reviled. You were aged about twelve at the time when you asked a priest why Jews are so reviled. His answer that it was because they killed Jesus did not make much sense to you even at the age you were then. Now you certainly cannot see what that has to do with the Blooms of Durham St. There was that boy in Loughgall of an appearance that was distinctly Mediterranean. It was the children calling their fellow Catholic 'jew-boy' in a tone of disgust that caused you to realise for the first time how labels make it easier for one group to imagine another group to be inferior - even a threat. To any existing economic or social problem there is a cause. Who or what could it be? It must be that lot that never seems to fit in. It seems that just looking different is enough for the whole person to be packaged in the eyes of another by just one word. Once so identified, all evidence to the contrary does not exist. For if it did, the sure will feel unsure again.

It is after mass that Mary is casually walking past Bathurst's Anglican Church when a woman she recognises as having been on her ship is bidding farewell to the minister at the front door.

"Minnie Mehafey! Mary Richardson. We were on the same ship."

"I remember. I am now Minnie Jackson. My husband has been transferred to Bathurst to be branch manager of the Commercial Bank of Sydney."

"And I am now Mary McCaffery. How could it be that I am discovering you at the steps of an alien church and not at Sunday mass?"

"I am no longer Catholic. To quote the Iron Duke: being born in a stable does not make one a horse. [see M13]

Stay calm. The Blooms denied their heritage due to the society they had to live within. Likewise, Minnie's husband and his family may have placed upon her a load of pressure of the like you were never subjected to.

There is some stilted chatting for three or four minutes before the parting with neither wishing to meet up again.

Goodbye Minnie. There will be no forgetting what seemed to be your sense of superiority.

BINDA AND RYDAL

With his employment looking shaky at the co-operative due to three bad seasons in succession, Dad has become worried. Nevertheless, even with so few shillings in reserve he still insists on his ale. It is there at the bar that he strikes-up with a lorry driver.

"There is a newly vacated position at the Binda sawmill on the Bathurst to Crookwell Road. Heading back to Binda carrying supplies for the farms springing up along the road. I can give you a lift."

An anxious wife learns from the next lorry to arrive in town that Dad is now working in the mill.

The children and you must join him as soon as the next rent is paid - yet the word 'apprehensive' hardly does justice to what is ahead. You have had more than enough experience of the roads here. Adding to the misery will be children who will be continually agitated.

Now on the road, the only traffic coming the other way are bullock teams carting milled timber that were once trees along the Abercrombie River. The driver notices the stress on his passenger's face.

"Lady. I have done the trip so often that I barely notice. I advise you to try not to be so aware of where you are."

You will not bother explaining to this man that a mother can never cease to be aware that she has agitated children. These hills go on and on. Mile follows mile follows mile. Always a bend in the road less than one hundred yards after the last. When meeting oncoming traffic at places where the road is especially narrow, manoeuvring is scary. Happily, only occasionally.

It is sometime the next day at yet another bend that there is the bellowing of animals as a dejected-looking man sits by the side of the road. About ten feet below him is his team, his wagon and his load.

It seems that when the rear wheel slipped off the side, the force of the shifting logs was enough to flip the two bullocks closest to the wagon over in a rotating motion with the closest chained to them following.

"Driver. Four are not moving."

"Broken necks lady. They are the lucky ones. The other four thrashing their heads about have broken legs. I have no gun. I can do no more than pick up the man and continue onto Binda."

Although after turning the first bend the bellowing can no longer be heard, the sound of it remains in Mary's mind until about one hundred yards from the mill when the bellowing of bullocks is driven out of her head by the chug-chug of a donkey engine and the high-pitched scream of the circular blade. As they draw closer, the children see a man who looks like Dad in the yard. They wave to him. When he waves back, a surge of love flows through his wife.

That man will take on any work to feed his family.

When all can come together, Mary already has a feel for what is going on here.

"Dad. The work is obviously not easy."

"Mostly to be cut is hard eucalypt. Then there is the dust getting into mouth and eyes. Playing hell with my back and shoulders is the lifting of logs onto the rollers and the sawn planks into stacks. Repetitive physical work always leads to problems. I had not thought of this common injury. When a man has money concerns, he does not look for reasons not to take up an apparently promising offer."

Most of the workers here look to be at least ten years younger than Dad. He was probably hired because he looks trim. The age of forty would not normally be a problem. In this type of work - it may be.

It is by the time their second girl Teresa arrives in the July of 1876 that the family had already squeezed into the only hut available on the site. For the six-year-old Bernard and the nine-year-old Patrick, the mother has two dilapidated books which have come her way. It is whenever she was reading the Water Babies or Westward Ho! to them, that an inner-voice intrudes on every occasion.

"This is not going to work. We must live where they can attend a real school." [see M14]

Since moving into the hut, life at a sawmill has not been a happy experience for anybody. Nevertheless, the family stoically hang in for two months after Teresa's birth before Dad makes an announcement.

"Going to resign. Take my chances in Rydal - a railway town."

There was no steady work to be had in Rydal. Just a week here and there - sometimes just a day here and there. For a family of seven, suitable accommodation was almost as big a problem as finding employment.

You know that it was far worse in the Old Country - but everything is relevant. Most in this country are doing better than we who have been living close to the edge for so long. [see M15]

It is in November 1877 while at Rydal that there arrives a letter from Rosanne Richardson stating that David had been killed while working on the railway at Jindalee. He had already been buried a month.

He was aged only thirty-five. An almost acceptable age to die in the Old Country. One can expect a better run over here. His son and three daughters leave you as an aunt to four you have never met. His eldest child aged only ten. Our siblings Henry, Teresa and John were still alive when David left Ireland. That is fifteen years past. So, who is alive? Who is dead? If alive - are they living in Loughgall? Canada? America? While you intentionally have not been thinking of the family to avoid the sadness of such a death-like loss when emigrating, now you know that you must write. Someone who knows what happened to them might receive the letter.

On the night of the day the letter from Rosanne arrived, that farewell at Loughgall comes back to Mary.

That feeling back then was more than the human mind can comprehend. Something like a collective death where you die on them and they die on you at the same time. Tonight, you will leave the candle to consume itself. The moment the room goes suddenly black, will mark the passing of your dear brother.

Over the next two years at Rydal, Dad could only get odd offerings driving carts to the railway station or working in the paddocks.

"Although life is easier now, I worry about the inconsistency of the work I am getting. I will aim at being my own boss. Unsurveyed land is being offered on terms at £1 an acre. I am going to apply."

"You know nothing about farming."

"True. But when I look elsewhere for possible opportunities, I see nothing. We abandoned our families in Ireland for a better life. We owe it to the abandoned to get that better life."

Those words 'we owe it to the abandoned to get that better life' remove any inclination this wife may have to question his decision.

TOWAC - THE SETTLING IN

It is on a day in October 1879 that the children and their mother are moving along the road leading to the mountain that dominates the southern horizon when seen from the town.

"Driver. Although the mountain does not look to be any more than a broad hill from the side we are approaching, the two tiring horses are saying that we have been steadily climbing for the last half-hour."

"Missus. We have been climbing the slopes of a mountain called Canobolas. Your selection is near the top. When winter comes you will discover what four-thousand-five-hundred feet above sea level this far from the sea really means."

"I assume that we have been passing those selections secured in the immediate years following The Robertson Land Act. Before I have even seen the McCaffery selection, I am envious of the prosperous looking properties we have been passing since leaving town."

"The best is always the first to be snapped up. That was some years ago following that change in property law. It will work out for you missus. Most problems tend to do that. Adaptation is God's way of assisting us in negotiating the testing environment we now must live in due to Eve's sin."

Not sure about that. Anyway, the pale-skinned McCafferys will be working land that only a few decades before was unknown to all but dark-skinned hunters and gatherers. You know before laying eyes on it that our selection is going to be very marginal. Those who got in early would probably describe it as rubbish.

It is when the mother is looking down at Teresa as she sleeps in her lap, that the driver's first words in a half-hour jolts her head upwards.

"We are here."

Dad and Pat are standing outside a structure that is as poor in appearance as a tenant-farmer's cottage in the most desolate parts of Ireland. Mary is seeing walls of split logs with earth stuffed in the cracks, a roof of overlapping sheets of bark secured by a frame of thin saplings tied together and glassless windows with wooden shutters hanging off leather hinges. It is as Pat and his father unload the gear onto the ground, that she steps inside onto bare earth. Weary after their journey from town, the children who are following are appearing to be bewildered by this turn of events in their lives.

"Children. We have lived in far better places. They were rented places. This humble dwelling is on land that we will eventually own."

Bernie is staring at the hut as if he is seeing this place to be worse than any he imagined.

"Son. I want you to see here a structure that was built by a man and his young son's own hands. I want you to see that within these walls and under this roof, you and your brothers and sisters will be growing to be young adults."

The driver who is behind has a question for the boy.

"Is any home entitled to be loved more?"

Mary smiles at him as she whispers:

"Thank-you."

Now on the ground outside are eating utensils, rocking chair, seven feather mattresses with pillows and a chest containing clothes and toiletries. The only food are four loaves of stale bread, a jar of jam, a leg of salted lamb, a twenty-pound bag of potatoes and a calico bag of tea leaves. Bernie and his mother pick up the food to carry it directly into the area set aside for cooking and eating.

At least this old table and the two old matching chairs have been made in a workshop. It seems that the tree stumps over against the wall are to serve as stools for the children. Those scars on the surface of the table that you are seeing are a record of meals prepared for children who are now adults and for adults who are now dead.

There is a room for the parents, one for the boys and one for the girls. The beds are milled boards nailed onto milled rails which tree stumps raise about a foot off the ground. Dad is looking embarrassed with what is on offer.

"I will have to take any work I can get from the neighbours in exchange for something to eat. It would not be until December that Pat and I can walk down to Nashdale. The orchard of my old boss Bob Armstrong at the cooperative is down there. As Bob has not bothered to pen pigs, the most recent windfalls are for anybody who wants them. We must try to be cheerful. Picture us digging our own carrots and potatoes out of the ground."

At this moment, the more pleasing picture in my head is a floor of wooden boards.

Just then a man is at the door with four hens in a wired coop.

"Your family might need these."

When George Plowman had left, Dad explained how Pat and he became friendly with the man and his wife Margaret.

"I suppose only to be expected. To get to the public road, the Plowmans must cut across our selection. You should like Margaret."

The thought of having a friend in that man's wife has suddenly lifted your spirits out of the hole they were in.

Dinner is over and all have washed in the nearby creek. The parents are on the two real chairs leaving the children the edge of the veranda to sit on. All are now watching the rapidly changing sky until the fading light passes the day over to the blackness of the bush.

Now suddenly feeling to be very alone in what has been a big day - the closing of it something like the end of your first day at sea - but it is at the end of this one that we have a glorious sunset. Always the sun is there to remind us of the power of our creator - but a merciful one? You have your doubts. Certainly, a testing one due to Eve's abominable female behaviour - as you have been recently informed.

Three-year-old Teresa is the first to fall asleep. Before long, all the children are in their beds leaving the parents to gaze into the flicker of the dying flames where thoughts wander. While the man follows his wife as she takes the lighted candle to bed, she is thinking:

Wonder when we can afford kerosene for a lamp? At least we have moved on from making smoky and smelly tallow candles to store-bought ones of wax.

As Dad is blowing out the flame, he says wearily:

"I hope the chooks are safe. Wire looks a bit thin."

In the silence and blackness of the bush, Mary is beginning to fall into the sleep of the emotionally exhausted when something inside of her whispers:

"It seems that Dad and you are doomed to work hard just to stay alive before dying with almost nothing."

A little down from the hut is the creek which borders where the school is to be built on a site that is as flat as a table. It is the day after arrival that Mary and her thirteen-year-old son Pat are soaking feet at a spot where water is swirling and bubbling over rocks. Pat does not raise his eyes from his feet.

"Dad has placed too much importance on me doing man's work. He must have had my labour in mind when he decided to take on this selection. In my head I saw he and I walking behind a horse as the plough turned over the rich sods. Now all I see ahead is the struggling to roll away logs, the digging out of rocks the size of buckets, the banging of an axe up against the hard trunks of the gums and the burning out of the stumps - all of that to get at some small patch of sloping ground."

"No inexperienced person can be blamed for the outcome of a decision made when circumstances require a decision to be made. You and I agree that mountain country seems to be telling delusional farmers that they should not be there - yet whatever it is telling us, it is here that we remain."

That night by a flickering candle Mary is looking at the children as the last drifts off to sleep.

In the Old Country every mother has fears for the future of her issue. Here one does not. Now you truly understand what pioneering is all about. You have said before that you felt that you understood. It is on this night that all doubt has been removed. Dad and you are not to prosper. We are to remain healthy to act as a springboard for the children. It is they who will be prospering. [see M16]

It is a battered ex-army Enfield that George Plowman is gifting to Dad after he purchased a replacement Springfield.

"You and I are the only poor blighters around the place who must put wildlife into the pot. What you can kill will make your family feel a lot better about yourselves. Life without meat is a life of little dignity in such a booming country. You will have no problem knocking over a wallaby a week. Quite a few are about now that the local farmers have got their farms operating and have tender lamb within easy reach."

As Mary is looking at the rifle, she suddenly realises something of historic significance.

The McCaffery clan's association with firearms has commenced after over two centuries of keeping clear of them for fear of being hung.

Later when she finds Pat and David fondling the Enfield, she informs the boys' father of what had been witnessed.

"It will be kept out of reach and unloaded. I can see the reason the boys are fascinated with this product of man's technical ingenuity. There is nothing mechanical in the house - not even a clock. At fifteen Pat should be trusted to hunt on the one condition that he is never to take any of his siblings with him."

It took only two hours after the decision that the gun be kept unloaded above the fireplace for Dad to change his mind.

"When both the eldest boys and myself are away - I want the Enfield ready to fire."

Men and their bloody guns. It is inconceivable that a mother could ever declare a war. On second thoughts. It is inconceivable that a woman could declare anything of any consequence. Her gender's place is in the background to catch the leftovers after the males have picked out what they want. Well - maybe not your man.

TOWAC - THE ESTABLISHING

It was in July 1880 with Margaret Plowman as midwife that a sixth child arrives. She is to be named Margaret.

You were disappointed with yet another pregnancy when life was so hard - but upon first sight of a newborn, attitudes always change. Now there is a joy in the family that the mother's ordeal is over. Big brother Pat seems especially to have taken to his new sister.

Almost coinciding with the new babe, Dad gets a paying job from a farmer within walking distance of their selection.

"Wilson Adams wants a stronger man to lift bags of potatoes onto his dray, cart that to the station and load that onto the train. There is a ten-shilling note in it for us - maybe more if he is happy with the arrangement."

You welcome the money - but am feeling a little humiliated. Real farmers do not drive drays carrying other farmers' produce to railway stations.

In June 1881 adjacent to the 97-acre portion already secured, another 40 acres is added under The Robertson Land Act.

It all looks promising on the map - yet nowhere on that additional forty-acre portion of rock, of fallen timber, of broken gullies and of trees collectively add up to one workable acre. As we will be forced to rely on hand tools to grow what we need to eat, maybe what we have now in the 97-acre portion is all we can manage.

What they eat from week to week depends on what can be stored. In the Old Country pits were dug so that perishables stored in late autumn would keep well into spring - but here where warm weather predominates, all the McCafferys have is a cooler which is a box with hessian sides kept permanently damp by a wick from a bowl of water. It is the evaporating water which keeps the air inside the box sufficiently cool when on the rare occasions that butter comes the family's way. Through dehydration in sun and air, thinly sliced fruit is preserved. To preserve meat, smoke from a hearth outside the house is contained by a cowl before being piped to the salted meat in a box. Potatoes and carrots are planted in spring to be harvested in late summer or early autumn. Special treats are the damaged and unsaleable fruit gathered off the ground under Armstrong's trees - but that can be only when in season.

Things are beginning to look up. Given time they had to - but the expectation of growing something that could be sold has well and truly departed the McCafferys.

There were two notable events in the year of 1882. One is that Pat eventually comes of age to handle the gun - the other is that he nearly kills Bernie.

"There is only a slice out of the skin. Another inch to the right would be deep trouble."

"If it can be patched up. Please say nothing to Dad."

You will not have to. No anger from him could have the same impact on your son's brain than this near-destruction of his own brother.

It is in January 1883 that the Towac Public School is taking in its new arrivals. The live-in teacher is a thin woman with a face that is saying that her body is not well.

"What are their ages, Mrs. McCaffery?"

"Eliza is ten. David eight. Teresa six."

"Glad you people have arrived. Your three bring the class up to twenty-five. To the administration of public schools, that seems to be a magical number required for a permanent teacher. I am fed-up with being shifted around."

This teacher must be aware of the humiliation you are feeling as here is a construction of the best milled timber put together by real carpenters laughing at the hut less than a thousand feet away. While huts don't laugh - children do - and their beautiful voices during their breaks are close enough to be heard.

Also in the stillness of the morning air is the ringing of the school bell at nine o'clock.

Although the Angelus is supposed to be recited at noon on the sound of the local church bell, you must assume that God will not care if the Angelus for you is at nine o'clock. St. Joseph's is a long way away - and you need the sound of a bell to feel right.

It is on Christmas morning 1883 that Pat gives Margaret a doll which he made from pieces of coloured cloth he picked up here and there. With her face beaming with delight, the child holds up the doll for all to see.

"Bee!"

Margaret sleeps with Bee which Pat has made large enough for his sister to feel that there is a real friend in her arms.

None in the family can fully understand the reason for Margaret's ability to tug at our heart strings. Maybe it is the eyes. When one looks into them, it is as if there is a peering into a soul as good as good can be on this Earth - and there another reason. As when struggling to survive, the staying of one step ahead of depression is a job in itself, it would seem to follow that when something special comes along it is grabbed with both hands. Witnessing the development of Margaret appears to be raising the whole family's emotional selves to another level. What this child does for the family goes to prove that we needed her. It seems that if she senses the family's valuing of her, a childish joyfulness will reflect that valuing. You cannot help but assume that hers is a promising beginning to a life which could be more rewarding than any in the miserable histories of both your family and of Dad's.

It is Margaret's fourth birthday on July 25, 1884 that becomes the occasion for the first party the family has ever staged. Cakes with sugar icing on top is to be provided by Mrs. Plowman. A dress with lace trim and ribbons for Bee is from the family.

The expression on her angelic little face when she is handed Bee in the new dress in the morning is what all in the family have been so impatient to see when retiring to bed on the previous night. This child reminds you of where Dad and your priorities must be. What really matters in life? Is it owning a thousand splendid acres of deep soil fed by permanent springs - or is it having happy and healthy children?

As the mother wants it to be a little more billowing than the sack-like dresses most daughters of selectors wear, it was at Christmas of that same year of 1884 that Mary puts Margaret in a dress stitched with a double layer of material at the waist. Now each time Margaret appears in the dress, her father says the same words:

"Our little one is looking so pretty."

That was the life that was. The new life began with a scream to haunt those who heard it to the end of their days. Margaret's dress is alight. Mary grabs an empty hessian bag to smother the flames. It is when she removes the bag that she is looking into eyes that are wild with terror. She carries Margaret into the house to lay the moaning child on her bedding to see a skin which looks as if it had been cooked. Pat runs to the school to find John Watts there with the sulky after he had already dropped some nearby children off at their homes. In the hospital the mother sits beside her moaning child to the time the lamps are turned down. A bed has been made up in a storeroom and meals are provided free of charge from the hospital kitchen.

You are calmer now after an experience that nothing from now on could ever match. For all the years that are to follow, you know that you will have an image of a billowing dress, of a burning stump, of a sudden gust of wind, of a scream and of a seemingly never-ending drive into town with a moaning child on your lap - not that you want to live at all after this eighth of March 1885.

After a bedside vigil for ten days, Dad says that a longer stay is pointless. It is as Mary is walking out of the hospital that she turns to look back at the building.

Your child is in there breathing but not moving. You can only hope that she is not much aware of her situation. As for yourself - you are so aware of your own situation that you feel that your heart may even give up trying to keep you alive.

Mary sees their child intermittently from then on as it is difficult to get into town and she feels that she has already said her farewell when she accepted that there was no hope. Margaret dies thirty-seven days after the fire with Pat by her side. Upon hearing of her passing, the mother walks down to the creek to a rock upon which on occasions she sits to contemplate. When seated she lifts her eyes to see the school children at play.

You were looking forward to your child's voice being one of those voices. Now the world of those children and their families goes on as before. It is our world which is now different.

As the mourners leave the cemetery on the following day, Dad turns to his wife.

"Why does God harm children? Was this punishment for some wrong that we are guilty of? If so, why not burn us? Our creator is beyond understanding."

Later that day, Mary is sitting with Margaret Plowman.

"Margaret. It was from the moment I heard Dad's lament that I knew that whatever respect he had for the teachings of Christianity is now gone. I am afraid that my grieving husband will live as he thinks fit and take his chances on what happens to his soul."

"I walked away from religion long ago for the same reason. I can understand how he now feels about our so-called loving God. You say that you have a grieving husband. Well, I am saying that he has a wife with a broken heart as only the hearts of mothers actually break." [see M17]

Now the famine years are coming back to you. It is the mother and not the father that holds the child as if was part of her own body. It is against her own body that she is feeling that there is no weight in that little being. It is against her own body that she is feels the icy-cold of its legs. It is she who is constantly aware of the blank eyes. It is she who hears every weak groan as pain grips its bowels. Your friend is right. Fathers' hearts grieve - mothers' hearts break.

As up here on the mountain it is only once a month that the McCafferys can get a lift into town in the Plowmans' dray, it is just once a month that Mary can step inside a church. Due to always arriving after the last mass, she can only sit in the church where a burning flame in a red glass bulb signifies the permanent divine presence in the tabernacle. [see M18]

While sitting here in the silence and watching the flicker of the flame, it seems that it is possible that you will meet up with Margaret again in an afterlife - but will Dad after so emphatically stating that since the loss of Margaret not to enter a church ever again?

> Aside: The picture on the front cover was in my possession for years before I learned of the terrible fate of her child. Now whenever I see that picture, I am reminded of the sorrow that Mary endured.

TOWAC - THE HANGING IN

On February 27, 1886 there appears in the New South Wales Gazette an announcement for all to see. Patrick McCaffery has lost his grant 'due to a failure to meet commitments'. That was the exact time by the calendar that the McCaffery family finally stops putting fanciful labels on themselves as farmers.

"It is not foolish to hope, Mary. It is human nature to hope. While there was something to aim at, we both would have been growing in the struggle." [see M19 and M20]

His attempt to ease the feeling of failure has not worked on you. You do not believe it is working on him. The grant is supposed to be paid for in three years. Nevertheless, Dad could have held it for as long as the five percent annual interest was paid. Even this in his disappointment of hopes being dashed, he was not willing to do. Our portion should never have been put up for selection to attract the dreamers. The whole one hundred and thirty-seven acres should have been included in the adjacent public reserve - yet here we will stay as this is where home is. While nobody is moving to push us off, life will simply continue as if nothing has changed. We will continue to grow a few vegetables, pick up odd jobs in the district and continue to put wild meat into the pot.

There is one unexpected positive. The introduced blackberry and rabbit proliferate as if they have found a heaven for themselves. The 'pests' are now becoming an important staple for this family along with the old standby of damper baked in a cavity scooped out of the dying fire made outside the hut with hot ash piled on top of the dough.

"Mary. Over the years you have become a whiz at damper-making."

"I humbly acknowledge that no skill is required if there is on hand cream of tartar, salt, sugar and pieces of dried fruit. If the firmness and the moisture is right - that is it! The drovers make them all the time when on the track. So, even a man can do it."

Somehow, being as he is married to a whiz, I cannot see Dad bothering.

It pleased the parents that the children seemed to have liked their schooling. That they did except for the one incident when her mother asked ten-year-old Teresa for an explanation for the marks on her legs.

"I was caned for talking in class - yet the girl I was talking to was also talking - and she was not hit."

"But there are several marks."

"As I did not make a sound with the first stroke, the teacher said that she would make me cry."

Those words 'I will make you cry' carry a lot of dislike in them. Your daughter being singled out is what you will not tolerate - even if by a valued neighbour.

> Aside: I muse on what the teacher's reaction would be when she said "I will make you cry" in 1886, if some voice from above told her at the time that those cruel words of hers would appear in a book in 2025. [see M21]

The following month was stressful for Mary as she hated the thought of a confrontation with the teacher. It is after another month free of incident has passed that she relaxes.

With the passing of time all disappointments are forgotten. No time should be wasted before forgetting this one.

Down from his six-hundred and eighty freehold acres on The Pinnacle, John Cole must drive past the McCaffery hut on the way to town. Rough mountain country as it generally is, John has about fifty acres that can be ploughed with a team. He is not a selector and he is not a squatter. This man is a real land owner after inheriting the freehold title from his father.

Although the Cole house is made from masonry and not split logs, it is very roughly built - yet inside there are woollen bedspreads with patterns knitted into them, laced curtains - and even a hand-painted vase. This man's property generates an income.

It was Eliza's seventeenth birthday. John had just left after having called in for a few minutes when Mary notices an unusually serious look on her daughter's face.

"I have turned seventeen. I can now marry John Cole."

Where did that come from? You had not noticed any more communication between John and Eliza than that between John and her siblings. However, her parents should not be that surprised. Every young woman's brain who had not already decided to become a nun was primed by some mysterious force to see only the positives in any man young enough and capable enough to father her children.

"Dad. There may be a better catch for the girl if she made a point of looking over the next two or three years."

"I can see no rational reason for objecting to her marrying into freehold property right now. The more years that slip by, the less likely there will be any match as good as the current prospective."

Putting it that way. You must agree with him.

On May 1,1889 Eliza flies from the nest.

With Margaret's death, Pat gone to work land of his own and Eliza now a wife - there are three holes in the family. Who will be next? [see M22]

Although the summit of the mountain was up there somewhere, it was at one relatively level place in the climb that David asks:

"How are you travelling mum?"

"I have no concerns - except that I just want this climb to end. What appears to be the top in the view from the road about a mile back does not seem far. Then what looks to be the top turns out to be a place where I see another top above that. David. Have you noticed that Bernie is doing no better than his old mum?"

"I have. There is more to this than exertion due to climbing. Something is organically wrong with his breathing."

With Bernie becoming increasingly breathless with little exertion, a doctor from town makes the diagnosis.

"One or more of his heart valves has been damaged. You told me about the time he went down with a severe throat infection when he was aged fourteen. The valve damage could be dated from that episode. Your son has rheumatic fever."

You know what is on the man's mind. Our son's condition has condemned him to an early grave. From here on, the ailing son is to become the focus of his mother's life.

It is in his final two months that Bernie is confined to his bed - and so light now that his father can lift him onto the toilet seat he has built on four legs. The day when he becomes unresponsive and his breathing erratic is a day of anguish for all. It was the next day that Dad wakes at first light to check on his son to find that Bernie is no longer breathing. As his forehead is already cold, it was sometime during the night the young man breathed his last breath. The father is gripped by a deep sadness that at the time of that last breath there was no family member beside him. Before waking Teresa and David, Dad gently wakes his wife and hugs her. Following David's ride on the school's horse into town to notify a doctor and an undertaker, a nurse and two men from the funeral parlour arrive in the same buggy. Until then, the family had been sitting by the body. The nurse listens to the young man's chest and says that she is sorry before calling to the two men standing on the veranda. Dad pulls Mary to him.

"We are not to see Bernie being carried from his home. Follow your mother and I out the back door."

Even if Eliza had given her parents a second grandson, the year 1892 was a bleak year during which Bernie was frequently on his parents' minds - yet there was one event to break Mary out of the bleakness. While only a material object, the black iron stove on the back of the dray was an announcement that a cake and a pie and a bread-filled future was before them. After the carter places two poles under the stove, the four males gently lower the stove onto a makeshift platform which is at the exact height of the hearth. When slid into the cavity one corner is levered up as a piece of flat iron is wedged to get a better level.

With the two kerosene lamps replacing the candles, matches replacing the tinder box before that - and now a stove, we McCafferys feel that we have stepped into the modern world - but before cakes comes the Staff of Life - bread! The cakes that follow will announce that a real homemaker is at home.

Although to buy and to sell is the way society works, for the McCafferys the capacity to sell anything seemed not to be part of their rural existence - yet on occasions, Mary wonders if they have been as unfortunate as she has so often assumed.

To habitually look at other lives in a positive way will create dissatisfaction. Even farmers like the relatively prosperous Adams are struggling to prosper over the long-term. When price for produce is high, it is because growing is difficult. When the price is low, it is because growing is easy. The farmer is stuck with harvesting whatever he decided to plant months earlier. If farming is a gamble, it is not a gamble for the merchant who buys and sells the product of the labour of others. In his privileged position he can switch with ease to whatever produce is the most profitable at the time. The accumulation of wealth of the richest men in the district is also immune to random plagues. The introduction of European species to remind one of home can be costly in unexpected ways - like the year when most of the district's cherries went into the bellies of English starlings.

As cakes mean eggs, the henhouse has been steadily built up with good layers producing a surplus. Hope turned into reality when the general store in Nashdale finally agreed to became a real customer with John Watts driving the school buggy delivering McCaffery eggs.

After continual struggle you were reluctant to believe that a corner has been turned - and John Watts is so willing to help us. That nightmare of a drive into town with Margaret affected him deeply.

All went well until six dozen eggs were broken when John's horse was spooked by a hare running across the road.

You had best not dare to think of corners being turned. Just take each day as it comes.

While food in a city has some variety, bush people tend to eat whatever is at hand. The McCaffery day begins with a breakfast of porridge made from Scottish oats and an egg on every day of the week. As Wilson Adams' wife has a churn, the McCafferys on occasions barter eggs for butter. In the absence of butter, the McCafferys have mostly the fat they call 'dripping' from the fortnightly roast to spread on bread. After dinner Dad has a ritual: tease out a plug of Yankee Doodle, slowly and carefully press it into the pipe, take a lighted taper from the fire - then get the thing going with as many sucks of air as it takes. As he might get three minutes of smoking before the process starts again, it is a ritual which seems to annoy David.

"Mum. I cannot see the point in such a struggle to relax."

Neither can your mum.

TOWAC. THE WINDING DOWN

It was after a Sunday mass in town that Mary notices Teresa and Nellie Madden's son David talking to each other.

What you are seeing must be a good thing. Our daughter must emerge out of her shell sometime - and it has been explained to her how things can go very wrong when young women associate with young men.

It was over the next six months that Mary knew that the young man and young woman had been in contact from time to time.

Cannot do much more than what you have already done to ensure that there be no problems.

Days went by with not much to distinguish one from the one before - that is until the day mother and daughter are sitting on the veranda of the Towac hut.

"Mum. I'm pregnant."

Calm down! You cannot be annoyed. Our own first-born was already walking when Dad and you married.

"David Madden?"

Teresa nods.

It could be worse. David is a tailor in town. Our family's lives would have been a lot more settled if Dad had a trade.

Thomas Patrick arrives on January 1, 1901 - the very same day the Commonwealth of Australia is signed into existence by Queen Victoria bringing the six colonies into a federation. While Pat and David are in town to welcome their little nephew and the new year with an ale, the mayor is delivering a speech to a crowd in the park in which he says that a new USA has been born. The boys can almost feel the surge of satisfaction sweeping through the audience as if the remotest of possibilities switches to become a probability - simply by somebody saying it. At the risk of ugly looks, Sinclair Plowman shoots down the mayor's speculation.

"We don't have the fertile soil. We don't have the water. We don't have the size of the population base - and we never will."

Pat had established on soil that was fertile a paying farm at Forest Reefs south of Orange. It was here that Dad had been since his second heart attack in early 1902.

You are missing him - but being under the care of Pat's young wife would be a more comfortable arrangement than this old woman could provide in a hut.

It was on the night before his last that Catherine goes to him after hearing his soft groans. When she finds him feverish, the foolish decision is to bring him to Orange Hospital. The outcome of a jarring fourteen miles taking nearly three hours to complete was that Dad dies soon after arrival. That was on May 25, 1902. It was as Pat pulled up in front of the hut that Mary knew that her husband had answered the creator's call. As she lay in bed that night, she has an image of a carter wearing fob-watch and chain and of her being introduced to him at the home of a friend of a friend. [see M23]

Of his childhood and his family, you have no knowledge except that his father's name was Bernard and his mother's name was Mary Rourke. You never saw him receive a letter nor send one.

It felt strange the next morning to see the sun rise on a day when there was no Patrick McCaffery in existence. After John Cole transports the widow into town the following day for the funeral, it is as she stares at the coffin provided by Pat and David that Mary is murmuring:

"Dad. If only you were alive to see the size of the funeral you got."

Although Mary had lived alone since Dad had his second heart attack, now with Dad dead, being alone became being lonely. That changed when this old woman finds a dog on the doorstep with tufts of fur missing and with the rib-cage and backbone clearly defined beneath the patchy fur.

His pleading eyes are saying that you need him in your life as he certainly needs you in his. To feed him just once would be to never get rid of him.

Mary stamps her foot.

"Get!"

He jumps back a little before putting his belly on the ground.

Your words might be incomprehensible to him. What he is reading in your face is not.

As his whimpering and begging eyes are beginning to affect her, she opens the door a little wider and turns back into the hut to pick up the darning of John's children's socks where she had left off. When she looks up about twenty minutes later, he is still sitting at the step.

Time to pick him up - bring him in.

That night Mary is feeling good about the situation.

Knowing that within this shelter there are now two hearts beating is having a noticeable effect on you. Are you really that lonely?

In the warmer months Icky sleeps outside the front door. In winter he sleeps at the base of the bed where he is always awake when Mary wakes - and that is when on occasions an inner-voice whispers:

"If you did not get that pleased look on that little face of his, you may not be able to face day after day alone."

Normally in summer the days are hot. Nevertheless, because of the dry air the nights are pleasant - but that is not to be on a night after a previous day of rain when the heat of the day is still lingering inside the hut. Icky is not around when Mary sets up her mattress on the veranda. She may have been lying awake for three hours when she looks up after hearing a chain dragging to see the jaws of a rabbit trap clamped onto front paw of her little dog. In the two seconds that her boot can compress the powerful spring, he is able to pull his paw out. It is the next day when the paw is very swollen that Mary is concerned that a bone may be broken. It is obvious after a further two days that he will make a complete recovery.

In all the years you have lived here, that night was the only night that you moved the bed outside - and what a horrible experience for your little mate as he must pull the spike up which holds the chain into the ground. He is only a small dog - yet he carries the weight of the iron trap for whatever distance it took to get home. Traps of every description are evil things - but what a coincidence! The one night when Icky gets caught in a trap is the one and only night you are sleeping on the veranda. God's finger in there?

After about eight years of the aging duo living together, Mary knew that the time of parting was not likely to be far away. It was not until she noticed that Icky was not eating much that she finally became unsettled. Two days later she wakes to find him breathing rapidly. With her in her rocker and he on his pillow, she does not want to move out of the hut. It is in the early hours of the next day that an old lady loses her little mate. That morning John calls in on his way into town and buries the dog for his exhausted mother-in-law. It is when looking down on the small grave that she admits to the man:

"I am feeling this loss more than the loss I felt when Dad died."

"You must not feel guilty. Your husband had been gone from Towac for over a year before he died. It has been just you and Icky for quite a few years since then. The more alone one is, the closer the bond to whatever living thing is in one's life."

Later when lying in bed, Mary is thinking:

The church teaches that none other than God's human creatures have souls. You now reject that teaching. When Icky looked into your eyes it was because his mind knew that behind that forehead another mind resides. That is human-like. If Icky does not deserve to go to Heaven - none of us do.

Eliza had been suffering from chest pain for maybe two months before the doctor felt a mass in her left breast. On the day following Eliza's and John's return from Sydney with an X-ray, the couple and Mary are sitting in the doctor's surgery and not liking the tense expression on the man's face.

"Eliza. I am afraid that you have a cancer. It has spread. It is now in your chest. It may have gone further than that."

"What can be done doctor?"

"Nothing."

While three pairs of eyes do not know where to look, it is with eyes looking slightly glazed that Eliza whispers:

"Can we go home now?"

It is when all are immersed in thought as they make for home that Mary becomes aware of one hoof hitting the ground in front of the other and of the bobbing head up front simply moving to where the driver points it. [see M24]

Inside that head is a brain which does not process the concept of death. Inside that chest is a heart within which no sorrow can reside. Whatever this animal was ever capable of feeling, it is due to what we humans have done to shape horses to meet our needs that he is now a machine.

The advice that Eliza's pain control becomes ineffective with repeated doses of morphine is of such a concern to John that he is thinking of the opium-smoking Chinese still fossicking for gold out there at Lewis Ponds - but it is only three weeks after the first morphine injection that she goes. That was on April 21, 1911. As John and Mary are looking down at the body, John mutters:

"This home cannot afford to lose what made it a home."

"And a home it still is, John. Although Tom and Pat have already left to find paying work and wives, there is still Dick, Sis, Maggie, Tess, Jack, Izae and Mick. My beautiful grandchildren are more than capable of making any house a home."

It was not long after she thought those words that it came time to feed two-year-old Mick - and it was then that the fullness of the position John was in strikes Mary. [see M25]

You see before you a child who will not only not have a mother - he will not be able to remember the one he had. Why does God take people early? Why Margaret after she had experienced only five years? Why Bernard after only twenty-one years? Why Eliza after thirty-nine years? If eternity awaits us - and if eternity has no end to it - then the period that is a life is of almost zero extent in comparison. Why not put us all on this earth for exactly three score and ten years with the heart stopping suddenly on the expiry date? Why is sickness and death inflicted so randomly? Why seemingly out of control when the creator is directing every event?

It is when the seventeen-year-old Dick Cole is in town at the showground that the sound of a beating drum leads him to a boxing tent where on display are two men in gowns - one of whom is an aborigine. Through a horn the promoter sends out a challenge:

"Who dares go three rounds of three minutes each with one of my men?"

The beat of the drum has set a match to Dick's warrior spirit.

"I'll take the abo."

The promoter asks the audience to give the young man a hand. While a few are clapping - most are simply looking to see how big the challenger is. Dick is then ushered into a canvas-walled enclosure at the rear while at the front a man exchanges a ticket for sixpence. As the prize is £3 - and the take is only one half of that - the promoter's man must dispatch the contender before going the distance. As the aborigine who has the name of Lucky is in his 'lucky' red corner, Dick must settle for the 'unlucky' blue. One of the promoter's men acts as Lucky's towelman. To the total stranger that volunteers to be Dick's, the boy's instruction is firm.

"Only if the ref pronounces me to be dead do you throw in the towel."

At the bell Dick comes out to meet his opponent as he is whispering:

"This is for you mum."

The distance for the unlucky Lucky finished before the second bell. Those next to the shocked promoter hear him exclaim:

"Christ! A knockout!"

It was after he relived the experience with his grandmother, that he left her thinking about what he had been saying.

For him to have knocked out an experienced man he must have developed some combat experience. It seems that the stoushes with his two older brothers were more numerous and more hard-fought than you had assumed. So, what do you know? One is that he has read everything that he could get his hands on since the world heavyweight bout in Sydney in 1908 and that a picture of the big negro Jack Johnson hangs over his bed. Another is that he does his training in his mind and reckons that if he gets his brain right, the movements of his body would follow its instructions. Another is that when awaiting the bell, he felt excited rather than nervous - and that is not what you wish to hear as his nemesis is surely out there. If he gets carried away by this first public success, it is inevitable that he will go on to get pummelled into the canvas - but what matters now is that the payout on this event together with some labouring work in the mason's yard will be enough to put your daughter's name carved into marble. You have a grandchild to be proud of.

When Dick goes to town on Saturday afternoon to return on Sunday, he calls in to replenish his grandmother's woodpile. Always she has a cake for him - and always he expresses the same concern.

"Gran. I do not like you to be living alone."

"Do not concern yourself about that. Life lacking human companionship is an adjustment that must be made - and a life of routine is so predictable that stress is negligible."

It was after he had left that the grandmother got to thinking about what she said to him about there being much to be said for a life of routine.

So, what can be said? It can be said that it is not a life in which nothing happens. When there is cloud about there are no two sunrises and sunsets which are the same. The first happening of the day is to get the stove going for the first cup of tea. The next is to put on the porridge. The next is the checking on the four chooks. It is at night that the flickering fire becomes the substitute companion. So, while it is not a life in which absolutely nothing happens - very little does happen. A significant turn for the worse came on the day when the school bell rang for the last time. From then on there were no more sounds of children at play. Now just bird calls and the distant baying of sheep and of cattle. Pleasant enough sounds - but not sounds of joy. There are the sounds of human voices when the Coles drop by on their way to town once a week for thirty or so minutes. At Christmas and Easter, you spend time with the families of Pat, David and Teresa in town after mass. Which for this old lady is nice when an occasional nice at her age will just have to do. [see M26]

AFTERWORD

It is on May 8, 1880 that Ann Madden is standing before a large open doorway and hearing female voices coming from a room at the dimly-lit end of the hall. She is a mix of apprehension and excitement as her left hand is gripping the handle of a port her father bought just for this occasion. Inside of it are a few things from the life of love she has left and which are now precious objects to be carried into a second life that is about to unfold. Upon pulling the bell the distant conversation abruptly stops. As someone is coming down the hall, in seconds she will step across a threshold that will separate her previous eighteen years from the rest of her life. So, when did this all begin?

Naturally introverted as a child, Ann hardly needs any companionship outside of her private world where Jesus hovers over her. When she becomes aware of the pregnancy of her mother, she is just as aware that it is Our Lord's divine will that a baby grows in a mother's belly at a time of his choosing. To witness the homebirth of her brother, David, horrified her - but to be worthy of Our Lord's kingdom mankind must suffer - even at the age of eight she understands this. When at age fourteen she announces that she wishes to be a nun, her mother is ecstatic as God blesses the home which gives-up a child to the church.

For the next four years the local church will supply reading material - 'The Lives of the Saints' being one example of the material chosen to keep the child moving towards an institutionalized life. When in church, she sees the representations in the stained glass of those so close to Heaven as to see visions and hear voices. [see N26] Then two years before she moves permanently into the convent, she attends a retreat where she will enter the next stage on the path to God.

So, what is the next stage on the path to God? That next stage in the hijacking of the impressionable young mind before it experiences what this world has to offer. For the week she and others are participating, they are not to speak to each other - not even in the dining room. Ann will sleep and sponge herself in her own cell. Her day's movements as per the program will be announced by a bell. She is only to attend religious services, read the prescribed literature and meditate. Each day of that week away from home the convent environment draws her deeper into its peace, deeper into its stability and deeper into its cohesion. She swallows the hook.

Her father is not as elated as his wife is by his daughter's calling. Nevertheless, he has no serious objection as he is recalling the Maddens' struggle to nurture eight children and the early loss of another. So, this call to Jesus may be preferable to their daughter having a similar struggle - or worse as more than one of the married men he knows is a drunken oaf. Now their daughter can hide from life with her Jesus where she will be safe. But safe from what?

The 'safety' that awaits her is no less than a barrier against all that threatens her commitments to humility, to poverty and to a system in which the core objective is to arrest normal sexual development by the driving into a young adult's brain the conviction that any feeling in the genital area is an 'impurity'.

As of human reproduction, Ann is to know no more than what she has already witnessed. She may even have gone to her grave believing that a baby grows in every womb at the time of God's choosing and that the man one calls 'father' is merely the person who generously agrees to provide for one's mother and siblings.

Today the situation as I have described it may be hard to accept as no person entering their teens would ever have Ann's infantile understanding of pregnancy - but what if sexual function is never discussed at home nor in the convent - and if all reading material is censored? How would Ann ever discover the facts? How could the inhabitants of a remote island more than a century ago know that there was land over the horizon if a boat never arrived?

Convent life is not an unpleasant life. There are housekeeping and gardening duties. There is the teaching of the farmers' kids in the small attached school - and there is the security of not having to make a weighty decision. Nevertheless, Ann is confined within a hierarchical structure which is there every hour of every day. Co-existing with what is almost a physical prison is one within the skull where resides a little homunculus whose function is to generate insecurity into the life of absolute security. This, the 'little person' does by maintaining the feeling of walking a tightrope above a black abyss. It is an illusionary danger oblivious to the reality of being victim to total mind control that is so complete that Ann must wear a black dress leaving only the face and hands exposed even in high summer.

In the archives of the convent there is a short summary of Ann's nature written by a fellow nun. I read that Ann was unable to control the boys in her classes. From that short statement I deduce that her self-esteem is low. I also have two letters written by Ann to my mother. One dated November 30, 1930 - the other dated November 18, 1931. The creases where she folded the paper are still there. As I read my mind is following the line of ink exactly as her mind guided her hand to shape the words - my mind and her mind in tune across decades. In each letter Ann promises to pray for all my mother's family. Then as a postscript she would add: 'Pray for me'. Poor Ann. A life sacrificed for God is still not a certain road to Heaven.

In 2014 I walk around those same grounds that she walked over for fifty-five years. While standing at Ann Madden's grave I am reminded that the first step into being absorbed into a total coercive situation is to have one's name taken away. The tablet states: Sr. Mary Edmund Died 21 June 1935.

Below is a letter written to my father by Mary Schmich.

Dear Ray

Your letter to hand pleased to see by it all well also Nell Les and Mill is back they come here now I am so pleased it is nice for me and they have alovely little kid bill is staying with Mill for a week it is apitty for poor Mill she went to Dr hoddy the other day he told her she wont live long if she dont get operated on he take it on but he says it is cerious her heart is bad he is giving her heart drops now she says her heart feels better he told her she has a normes apses carnt be cured with out a operation she is afraid of corse one carnt blame her it be one way or the other he wants her to go in now but she is hanging of I don't blame her in away it is cerious Dr said it was he would of cured her if she had him first the other Dr done nothing they wouldent take it on once they opened her told Les she die under anace tick hoddie don't be leive in giving the sleeping pills what do you think of it Ray do you think she ought to go to Sydney to be done let me know all about it when you write my opinion it be one way or the other find out all about those apses it is anormes one he says it goin acros to the write side not draining much now I herd when it stops draining it is dangerous she wouldent live long she hasent much life in her very (cannot decipher the next word)
     I suppose she is werring poor Mill

Love from Gran
Write soon
dont notice me not writing

*befor as I have been
very buisey*

Written in the margin:
poor Mill Ray you asked me about the photo bill had it showed it to nell before I could say any thing did she mension it to you there was nothing said that might wory I think took it in good part I hav ent seen them sence gone for a holi day I think

The third page was written on the back of the first page and the second page had writing in the margins - even though the back of it was blank. In addition to lack of reading material, how much illiteracy in those days was due to the lack of reading glasses? I once saw Teresa reading a newspaper through a piece of broken spectacles held up to one eye.

NOTES

Some of these notes would only be of interest to my family. I put them down here as I do not want the information lost. Family histories must be stitched together by guesses as Ireland was one of the most primitive places in Europe. Pregnancies out of wedlock were occurring everywhere. Deaths were also occurring everywhere leaving widows to remarry just to survive and widowers to remarry to mother their children.

[N1] As Ireland had been part of the United Kingdom since 1801, Westminster was obliged to introduce a welfare program for the hungry families of the Irish tenants. It was one the landlord had to pay for. The landlord's solution was to get rid of the tenants. The outcome was little or no effective welfare.

[N2] There is nothing supernatural happening here. From the girl's emotional state has emerged a lucid dream.

[N3] For reasons which today seem bewildering, poverty was at the time almost regarded as a crime. What was called 'welfare' seemed to be designed to cause the inmates of the workhouses to feel bad about themselves.

[N4] Excavations in 2009 of the burial ground of the Kilkenny workhouse which housed the Campions uncovered the remains of 545 children. Most had stunted skeletons and teeth diagnostic of scurvy.

[N5] To the country you are leaving you are an emigrant. To the country receiving you, you are an immigrant. As the New South Wales government is funding the passage, the emigrant becomes an immigrant as soon as he or she boards the ship.

[N6] An Ellen Campion is recorded to be able to read, that she paid only £1 and that her conduct was good. The ship's surgeon kept detailed records on all the emigrants. Almost all such records have been destroyed by those who could not imagine that anybody in the future would be interested in the lives of the 19th century working class. Outside of a few isolated reports here and there, little remains beyond the passenger lists. Nellie's ship arrived in Sydney after only 86 days out of Liverpool. On February 11, 1853 the ship was finally anchored in Sydney harbour proper after spending five weeks off the Quarantine Station. From the archives of Lynne Bell Sanders: *The arrival of the BEEJAPORE with over one thousand passengers, at a time when the Quarantine Station could accommodate 150 persons, triggered a new building phase. As a temporary measure, the hulk HARMONY was purchased and moored in Spring Cove as a hospital ship. The BEEJAPORE was an experiment in trying to reduce migration costs by using two-deck vessels, and the outcome was judged not to be a success. Fifty-five people died during the voyage, and a further sixty-two died at the Quarantine Station, from the illnesses of measles, scarlet fever and typhus fever. The majority of the passengers and crew had to be housed in tents. The biggest impetus for change came not so much from a concern about poor housing, but rather a concern for the morals of the married women and the 200 single women let loose in the bush that represented the undeveloped station at that time. The resulting changes to the station, besides the use of the hospital ship, included the construction of a barracks for the single women in the former Sick Ground, surrounded by a double fence with a sentry stationed between them, to prevent communication with the women. Two new buildings were built in the Healthy Ground, each to house sixty people, with verandas for dining. The original burial ground was levelled and the grave stones [though not the dead] removed to the new [second] burial ground, thus further removing the burials from the view of the Healthy Ground. Quarters were built for the Superintendent.*

[N7] The human brain is exceptionally accommodating to music. I know this as I only need to hear the first three or four notes on the radio of a song which I have not heard for 40 years to know what is coming next. Music is the source of so much pleasure in most lives that it is not realized that only since the coming of instruments which produced a range of notes that the music we now enjoy was possible. So, for the 300,000 or so years that modern man is thought to have been in existence, it was only from about 4500 years ago that we began to have the music that the modern brain had been waiting to receive in all that time.

[N8] To the native all is relived through the enduring pattern of birth, survival and death. The pattern was set against a background of repetitive cycles of a changing moon, of the length of the day and the associated change in the average temperature and of the seasonal changing of the plants.

[N9] Nellie's fears for the future of the natives were very relevant. Here is an extract from the Sydney Herald of November

7, 1838; *This vast country was to them a common. Their ownership, their right, was nothing more than that of the emu or kangaroo. They bestowed no labour upon the land – and that only it is which gives the right of property to it. Where, we ask, is the man endowed with even a modicum of reasoning powers who will assert that this great continent was ever intended by the Creator to remain an unproductive wilderness? The British people took possession and they had a perfect right to do so under the Divine authority by which man was commanded to go forth to people and till the land.*

[N10] As I child I would occasionally hunt rabbits with my father. At one time we came across young men with rifles seemingly out to shoot at anything for thrills. I now realise that a century earlier, if such men on horseback came across an aboriginal camp, they would dare each other to kill one of the people before them. Rather than appearing to be 'chicken', one would shoot to kill. Not only could the men simply ride away - but the black man would have neither the confidence nor the language to report the incident to the police. This is what the Rev. William Yate said to the Select Committee on Aborigines in 1835: *I have heard again and again people say they were nothing better than dogs and that it was no more harm to shoot them than it would be to shoot a dog when it barked at you.* We know of a few massacres which could not be kept off the record - but in the gun-revered culture of the 19th century, I am convinced that thousands of aborigines were murdered for the thrill of the kill. This assumption is supported by the enthusiasm of young men seemingly desperate to enlist in the first months of WW1. As Germany posed no threat to Australia, the attraction was to fondle your very own rifle with which you could reach the ultimate pinnacle of manhood by killing another man

[N11] When Europeans arrived, they failed to read the evidence staring them in the face. It was the 65,000 years' worth of evidence of the only sustainable way to live - but now the Indigenous communities seem to be collapsing in on themselves. The data tells us that an Aboriginal woman living in aboriginal communities today is 35 times more likely to be hospitalised due to domestic violence than that of a non-Aboriginal. The violence is alcohol fuelled. The alcohol abuse in turn is driven by the perception of hopelessness. Aboriginal children attend school when they feel like it. 'Solutions' are put forward from time-to-time which amount to nothing. Even after over 230 years of European settlement, the Indigenous perception of normality remains out of sync with that of the European. The reason is clear enough. The foundation of black communities was the natural environment free of any mark of industrial man. In this 21st century almost all of that has vanished.

[N12] Maybe it should not be so hard to believe. A government surveyor in Victoria is supposed to have measured in the 1870s a log of Mountain Ash to be about 150 feet more than the height of the tallest living Sequoia in North America. Although botanists say that such a height is highly unlikely, I remember reading about Victoria's monster log stated as a fact in an old geography book for English schools.

[N13] April 26, 2015 was the 160th anniversary of the marriage. Because the chancel and sanctuary are as they were in 1855, I attend the service to mark that anniversary. Even though it was a Sunday, I ask nobody in my family to accompany me as I know none would be interested. Nellie's maiden name appears as Champion and not Campion on the marriage certificate. Then on the various certificates that follow for herself, Paddy and children, her maiden name appears as Campon. Camfron. Camplin. Campan. Camphin. Canfrin. Canfred. In total eight variations on Campion! The carelessness in recording details of the lives of the working class frustrates today's researcher.

[N14] In the police recruitment record one in seven has a 'slovenly' or 'untidy' appearance. Paddy is recorded as being one of the 'untidy in general appearance'. As the dates of recruitment approach the 1880s, all are of at least good appearance. This is in keeping with the earlier recruits still being affected by their hard youth in Europe while the later recruits had been moulded by the wealth and vision of an emerging nation.

[N15] For a man to whip another man he must be seeing the life-form tied to a post before him as being less than human. Seemingly recalcitrant convicts whose lashes totalled hundreds over a period of years were likely to be of abnormally low intellect and vulnerable to be seen as less than human. The mental retardation can be due to the mother being malnourished when pregnant. Added to that handicap is the infant's developing brain being both malnourished and lacking stimulation in the form of pictures in books and coloured objects to play with. There was also an exposure to a limited vocabulary. A wide range of words is necessary to analyse one's own perceptions of reality. Horrifying conditions within the orphanages would also produce troubled minds. This is what the Anglican pastor and magistrate Samuel Marsden had to say at the time about the type of man who built the road over the Blue Mountains; *The number of Catholic Convicts is very great - and these in general composed of the lowest class of the Irish nation who are the most wild, ignorant and savage race that were ever favoured with the light of civilization. Men that have been familiar with every horrid crime from their Infancy. Their minds, destitute of every principle of religion and morality, render them capable of perpetrating the most nefarious acts in cool blood. As they never appear to reflect upon consequences, but are always alive to rebellion and* mischief, they are very dangerous members of society. No confidence whatever can be placed in them.

[N16] In 1836, the great Charles Darwin returning from his observations in the eastern Pacific stood on the same spot that Nellie and Madge stood. He writes: *Stupendous. Magnificent. Profound.*

[N17] The road the Maddens followed in 1857 had been rerouted and much improved with the notorious descent off Mt York (which required logs to be dragged behind the wagons as additional braking) bypassed. Nevertheless, it was still a torturous road. From a letter back home by Sophie Stranger: *As there are no such roads in good old England, you can form no idea how bad these are.*

[N18] From 'The Empire' November 17, 1857; *I have seen the drunkards of a London gin palace. They are, comparatively speaking, patterns of virtue by the side of a bush drunkard. It is not an uncommon sight to see a man on the veranda of a public-house in that beastly state of unconsciousness. They drink, as it were, without knowing it. They fight and roll about till they cannot stand. Then they lay huddled together like so many hogs wallowing in their filth. One occasionally waking up and calling with an oath; 'Who is going to shout?* ('To shout' means to buy beers for all present.)

[N19] Research into family history tends to suck the curious down a rabbit hole. Even the uncovering of a single scrap of information is felt like a win. One scrap of information I uncovered in my general research was the census of 1901 stating that Nellie's spinster daughter Johanna was sharing my mother's family home. This then brought back a memory of my mother telling me that when her parents were separated - but still living under the same roof - she observed Johanna spying on her mother and reporting back to her father. My mother hated her for that. Nevertheless, Johanna was family and the only way I could make some form of spiritual connection to this person I had not seen even a photo of was by standing outside her last address as stated on her death certificate. It was all for nothing. The entire row of houses on her side of the street had been replaced by warehouses. The young see only progress. To the old there is something pitiless about heavy machinery breaking an old house up into rubble in mere minutes.

[N20] Only the material at hand can be worked with. So, wide gaps in time appear in this book.

[N21] The discoverer of the first gold in Australia was Lawrence Hargrave. He decided against keeping his find a secret and to write a letter to the governor. It was a letter that was to have world-wide consequences. He wrote that letter in Guyong's inn.

[N22] In 1862 in H division under Superintendent Edric Morisset, were one inspector, two sub-inspectors, six senior sergeants, nine sergeants, fifteen senior constables and eighty constables. So, there were 5.5 constables to each senior constable - yet after 13 years, Paddy was still a constable. Paddy need not have been so respectful of the men on top of the pyramid. The inspector was Frederick Pottinger who was continually mired in controversy and who accidentally killed himself. This incompetent's number two position in H division was due to him being an Eton-educated baronet.

[N23] In his will of 1893, Paddy left Nellie a life-interest in his property (meaning that she cannot be pushed out until she is ready to go). The property was to be legally divided between David and Phillip. In the will he says that Phillip is supposed to be in Queensland. So, although he has lost all contact with Phillip, he wants to remain his father by recognising in his will that he has two sons. Also, there would be no likelihood of his sons becoming friends if one was the sole beneficiary of the father's estate. The complication of the missing son delayed the settling of the inheritance by the Public Trustee until 1932.

[N24] Paddy and Nellie must be in Orange Cemetery somewhere. Burial records were lost in a church fire before the local council kept cemetery records. I could find Nellie's obituary. I could not find that of her husband who died on the 9th of April 1895. A copy of each day's local newspaper was kept in a basement where a flood destroyed them. Although hundreds of copies were printed each day, nobody thought to keep two copies and store them at separate locations.

[N25] Nellie died on the 29th of September 1898. This appeared on October 7, 1898 in 'The Western Champion'. *The death is announced of Mrs. P. Madden a resident of Orange for 25 years at her residence Moulder Street, from influenza after an illness of seven weeks. She was the relect of the late Patrick Madden who died three years ago and leaves a family of six daughters and two sons. Her age was 61.*

[N26] There is an alternative interpretation. The church has put halos around the heads of schizophrenics.

[M1] Sis was John Cole's teenage daughter. For some reason she was not living on the farm with her father where she could have helped with the younger children following the death of the mother - and now slept with Teresa. One night, Teresa hears a faint cry. She pulls back the bedclothes to reveal a newborn boy. One can only wonder how many girls in those days wearing sack-like dresses could not communicate their concern to anybody for what was happening in their bodies.

[M2] Protestant gangs were determined and looking to attack. Catholic gangs were formed to hit back in defence. In the Battle of the Diamond near Loughgall on September 21, 1795 there probably had been young Richardson men in the Peep O'Day

Boys, and young men from Mary's mother's family (the McNeices) in the Defenders. The Peep O'Day boys had the muskets and the high ground and suffered no casualties. Later 7000 Catholics were driven from the county. The match that lit the fuse was competition for jobs in the linen industry in Ireland which was suffering due to the mechanisation of the cotton industry in England. The Order of Orange which still marches in Belfast each year to commemorate a Protestant victory in 1690, was founded in an inn in Loughgall.

[M3] I was uncomfortable with this piece. However - that is the warped way a significant proportion of priests behaved. One incident I learned of was when a radio personality (John Doyle) said on the ABC that he left the church as a teenager after a priest asked him in the confessional if he has sexual feelings for his mother.

[M4] To avoid England was good advice from the priest. In the one year of 1846 about 280,000 Irish landed in Liverpool. The lack of food and shelter and the degree of hostility which awaited them can be imagined. The exodus was due to a famine in a land that was exporting grain and meat produced by the hungry working on the tenancies owned by the English landlords.

[M5] From 1830 Westminster became anxious to raise the literacy level throughout the kingdom. Mary would have learned to write in elementary school. However, with nothing to write from then on, the skill was lost. Having mostly not lived in anything but a one room cabin, rural Irish imports had the reputation of being generally 'near-useless' in domestic service - yet the passenger lists recorded them as 'house servants'. In truth they were imported as potential baby-makers. Mary was most probably hired because Sarah was there to teach her.

[M6] Twenty years later the population was 230,000.

[M7] At the time of Mary's arrival, Sydney was only 70 years old. To me the contemporary photographs show the development over that period to be astonishing. When Charles Darwin visited Sydney in the 1830's, he was so impressed with what had developed since 1788 (when compared to Spanish and Portuguese South America) that he wrote; *I felt proud to be an Englishman.*

[M8] The beach became public in 1882 - but only males were permitted to bathe in public at the time.

[M9] Under the Remittance Regulations the cost of passage was £14. As Mary only paid £7 for David, her father must have paid the balance of £7. The hopeful Mary has paid James' full fare of £14.

[M10] In her new country, Mary seems to be a liberated woman. What was courting back in Ireland like at the time? It did not extend much beyond assessing local availability as parents and church almost ordered those of marriageable age to marry. It was not until about the turn of the 20th century when working class young men could afford bicycles that the range of choice (and the distribution of genes) was extended. The church ensured through its policy of sexual terrorism that a pregnant unmarried young woman was a woman fit only to be cast out. The Irish emigrants believed that they were fleeing English oppression. When they got to their destinations, they discovered that they had also fled much of their church's power to oppress them.

[M11] William Howitt in 1855, when the diggings were at their peak, had this to say: *We had quietness and greenness and deliciously cool water. Sweet and clear. But this quietness and greenness cannot last. Prospectors will quickly follow us and all these shy banks of the creek will be rapidly and violently invaded. The hop-shrubs will be burnt. The bushes along and in the creek cleared away, the trees on the slope felled and the ground dug up for miles around. The crystalline water will be made thick and foul with gold-washings and the whole will be converted into desolation and discomfort. A little while and its whole course will exhibit nothing but nakedness, heaps of gravel and mud.*

[M12] The luckiest were able to contribute to the building in Braidwood of the most impressive small church I have ever seen. Prayers for a lucky strike may have ensured good attendances. I went to Braidwood hoping to find traces of the diggings around the creek. I found none.

[M13] The Iron Duke referred to by Minnie was the Irish-born Duke of Wellington.

[M14] Mary may have sought out replacement books if she knew that the author of the two books (Charles Kingsley) referred to Irish Catholics as *white chimpanzees*.

[M15] Events that I know are missing from Winifred's recordings I am tempted to add myself - even if of a trivial nature. One is that in September 1876, Teresa's birth was registered at the Hartley courthouse 20 miles distant by road from Rydal and 120 miles by road from Binda. So, the registration of the child was necessarily delayed until the family was at Rydal.

[M16] Mary was counting on the next generation being prosperous. She was one generation ahead of herself. All her surviving children had to work hard. It was Mary's grandchildren who enjoyed the 'good life'.

[M17] The statement by Margaret Plowman reflects the practice in those days that put a barrier between father and children. The barrier between father and daughter was the father's authoritative role as provider and protector as distinct from nurturer. The barrier between father and son was due to the male perspective of survival of the fittest. The laying of the belt across a son 'for his own good' was a very common practice.

Such cultural norms hindered the establishment of a strong bond with a father which today most fathers enjoy. If Margaret Plowman believed that fathers' hearts do not break it would have been the perception of the mother as the one true source of deep love.

[M18] In her aging, Mary seems to have grown closer to the church since the uncomfortable experience with Fr. Grogan. This is to be expected as she is seeing a bigger picture in which an organisation is more than the behaviour of one individual.

[M19] The still unsurveyed McCaffery grant was taken over by Sinclair James Plowman and Daniel Sinclair Plowman in 1891. The records show that up until the 1891 takeover, son David had some type of legal interest in the top 40 acres. It was not until December 17, 1909 that the Plowmans held full and unconditional (Torrens) title of a fully surveyed portion of land. By then, Dad had been dead for seven years. As it seems that the Plowmans never intended to do anything with the basically worthless land, Mary was permitted to stay on in her hut. Today there is a tearoom a few yards down from where the McCaffery hut stood.

[M20] Steele Rudd opened his book titled 'On Our Selection' with these beautiful words; *To you who gave our country birth; to the memory of you whose names, whose giant enterprise, whose deeds of fortitude and daring were never engraved on tablet or tombstone; to you who strove through the silences of the bush-lands and made them ours; to you who delved and toiled in loneliness through the years that have faded away; to you who have no place in the history of our country so far as it is yet written; to you who have done most for this land; to you for whom, in the march of settlement, in the turmoil of busy city life, few now appear to care; and to you particularly, good old dad, this book is most affectionately dedicated.* (The writer said 'good old dad'. There was also good old mum.)

[M21] Teresa only mentioned this 'I'll make you cry' incident and did not elaborate on it as I did not ask her to. What she did say at the time was that I was lucky to be going to a Catholic school. While she preferred to believe that such abuse does not occur in Catholic schools, the cane was used liberally on boys who had mental blocks (of which I was one). In retrospect I realise that most members of the religious orders of brothers (e.g., Marist, de la Salle) had no desire to be school teachers. Their only desire was to be cloistered away from society - but the church needed them to staff its schools.

[M22] After Eliza's marriage, the fourth hole was created by Bernie's death in 1891. Teresa at age 24 became the fifth hole when she married David Madden from Orange in 1900. They had four children. David McCaffery at age 34 became the sixth hole when he married Catherine Norris from Coffee Hill in 1908. They had six children. Pat at age 31 had already married Catherine Rapley from Springside in 1898. They had eight children. A formal witness to David's marriage was a Mary Jane who was the eight-year-old daughter of Pat. Back then the church seemed to think that reaching the age of reason was a sufficient qualification to bear witness.

[M23] I don't know the name of the newspaper, as what follows was a cut-out. *We regret to record the death of Mr. Patrick McCaffery, an old and respected resident, which occurred in the Orange Hospital yesterday from pneumonia. He was brought in from his son's residence, Forest Reefs, on Monday last, suffering from the complaint, and was placed in the hospital, when it was ascertained that the disease was of a malignant character. The deceased gentleman, who was 65 years of age, leaves a widow and a grown-up family of two sons and two* daughters. He settled in the district about 26 years ago, shortly after his arrival in the colony. He took up a farm at Canobolas where he resided for many years. His funeral will leave the residence of his son-in-law Mr. P. Madden, Moulder Street, at 2.30 today and St. Joseph's Catholic Church at 3 o'clock. Mrs. Hale has been entrusted with the mortuary arrangements. The last rites will be conducted by the Rev. J.J. Ryan.

[M24] That we reduce horses to machines came home to me when I was with a group of walkers in central Australia. We were silently and slowly approaching a dozen or so wild horses drinking from a pool at the bottom of a very steep hill. Although we made no sound or movement that could be seen, the animal on guard gave the signal to bolt. This they did as one as they thundered up that steep incline. Contrast this with the cart horse who each morning is backed into his cart for another day of mindless pulling in the direction his head is pointed.

[M25] Upon cutting out the other children, John Cole left the 680 acres to Mick and Jack - yet Jack ended up sole owner. Teresa told me that land rates were owing on the estate which Jack could discharge and Mick could not. In a record provided by the descendants of Eliza's daughter, Tess, one story is that Jack allowed Mick to have a hut which Mick walked away from over a dispute with Jack relating to the shooting of a dog. To simply walk off over an accident indicates there being bad blood between the brothers due to the outcome of the inheritance. The 680 acres has been lost to the Cole family. It is now a pine plantation.

[M26] Mary died on the 14th of January 1916. I don't know the name of the newspaper. What follows is from a cut-out. *A self-reliant old resident passed away on Friday evening in Mrs. McCaffery of 'Towac'. She was a native of Armagh, Ireland, and came to this state about sixty years ago. After a residence in Braidwood, where we understand she was married, and in*

Bathurst, she came with her husband to Towac forty years ago, and there she resided till the fatal illness overtook her. She was removed to the hospital with an attack of pneumonia from which she recovered, but was further attacked with inflammation of the tonsils, which carried her off. She was eighty years of age.

Born in the 1830s and emigrating in the 1850s, Winifred Condon was a compatriot of two of my great-grandmothers. Other than that - I know nothing about her. Nevertheless, I have imagined her to be a science prodigy who was born into an Ireland which was steeped in a superstition that was not far above that of darkest Africa.

To lift her out of the mire, I have her firstly in conversation with an uncle who is an enlightened school teacher fearful of any outside his family discovering how he really thinks. Then as a secretary-cleaner for a physician who she discovered was not the ordinary medical man as he discovered her not to be the ordinary secretary-cleaner. Then as the wife of an uneducated self-made man who became enlightened by just one book: Darwin's 'Origin of the Species'. Then as an acquaintance of a university lecturer in mathematics who she met in a casual game of chess.

Highly contrived as this may be, I felt the need of a novel built around such lateral-thinking people to pass a message to my grandchildren that could be life-changing for them. That message is that you exist for a moment in a time that may be infinite on a ball-shaped lump of matter suspended in a space that may be infinite - and it is a worthwhile thing to know how you appeared on that ball and how you are able to exist on it.

Although the story is basically of Winifred's learning experiences, it was in the writing of this book that became a learning experience for me. Hence the twenty-first century updates.

www.ingramcontent.com/pod-product-compliance
Lightning Source LLC
Chambersburg PA
CBHW030257010526
44107CB00053B/1744